# LIFE

BRAVING ADULTHOOD WITH BIBLICAL PASSION

# QUEST

CARY SCHMIDT

First published in 2007 by Striving Together Publications, a ministry of Lancaster Baptist Church, Lancaster, CA 93535. Striving Together Publications is committed to providing tried, trusted, and proven books that will further equip local churches to carry out the Great Commission. Your comments and suggestions are valued.

Striving Together Publications
4020 E. Lancaster Blvd.
Lancaster, CA 93535
800.201.7748

Cover design by Jeremy Lofgren
Layout by Craig Parker
Edited by Amanda Michael, Sarah Michael, and Danielle Mordh
Special thanks to our proofreaders.

ISBN 978-1-59894-075-6

**Printed in the United States of America**

# DEDICATION

To my wife,
Dana

My heart is overwhelmed that God
included you in my "life quest"!
Thank you for being my best friend
and my life's companion!

# ACKNOWLEDGMENTS

A book is a major project that involves a large team of people.

My heart is deeply grateful to Pastor Paul Chappell for allowing me to serve at Lancaster Baptist Church and to participate in the Striving Together Publications Ministry. More than these things, I thank him for being a wonderful Pastor to my family on a weekly basis.

Thank you to Josh Irmler, Amanda Michael, Sarah Michael, and Danielle Mordh for your time in reviewing and creatively critiquing this manuscript as it was being written. Your input was invaluable and much appreciated.

Thank you to the group of young adults that pre-read this book before it went to press. I appreciated your input and encouragement along the way.

Thank you to our volunteer ministry proofreaders. This incredible group of people gave hundreds of hours to proof and re-proof this book prior to printing. I am thankful for your heart to serve the Lord with your sharp eyes and editing skills!

Thank you to Jeremy Lofgren for your help with the cover design and to Craig Parker for your excellent layout skills.

Thank you to the young adults of Lancaster Baptist Church—Dana and I consider you our best friends. Your heart for the Lord and your passion to serve Him proves that not every young adult is a "twixter," and there is great hope for the next generation!

# Contents

*continued...*

# PREFACE

*from Dr. Paul Chappell*

The book you are holding in your hand is a one-of-a-kind, highly needed resource for young adults and those who care about them.

As I read through the pages of *Life Quest*, I was encouraged and challenged by the biblical insights of the author.

Cary Schmidt labors faithfully each week to serve over eight hundred teenagers and young adults and their families. He is not writing as someone who used to be involved, but as someone who is totally immersed in servant-hearted ministry of our Lord Jesus Christ.

Cary's techniques do not involve constant repetition of radical ideas, activities, and lightweight story telling-type messages. While he enjoys having fun with young people, he has consistently nurtured the hearts of people through the teachings of the Word of God, and today hundreds of these young people are actively following their Saviour in all walks of life, including many who serve the Lord in places of ministry around the world.

I am not only encouraged about *Life Quest* because of my knowledge of the author, but because of the great need it addresses in American society today. Many recent surveys have indicated that young people between the ages of eighteen and thirty are missing out on "some of the best years of their lives."

Cary challenges these young people to move past their fixation with folly and to become fully engaged followers of Jesus Christ. The reason this is so vital is because even some of the best churches in America today are losing the young people who graduate from their high school youth groups at an alarming percentage rate.

Parents, youth pastors, and Christian leaders looking for a resource to help this lost generation will find *Life Quest* filled with answers, practical challenges, and emotional helps just for them.

If you are a young adult, let me encourage you to read this book with a pencil and paper in your hand. As your heart is challenged, you may want to write down thoughts that you want to ponder and apply to your personal life.

If you are a parent or a Christian worker with a passion to help young adults, you will want to have a paper and pen also. There will be many principles, illustrations, and biblical concepts on these pages that will help you in the work God has called you to do.

May your quest for the abundant life promised by Jesus Christ be greatly encouraged by the reading of this book!

# PREFACE

*from Dr. Don Sisk*

L*ife Quest* is a fascinating book! Cary Schmidt writes from a great knowledge about his subject, and he addresses a very prominent yet little discussed subject. I began reading this on a long plane trip, and the trip was shortened because of my total concentration on this interesting book.

Cary is a very gifted writer who writes with passion about the age group to which he has committed much of his adult life. He has faithfully served as youth pastor to a large, aggressive, and growing church. Cary has grown with the church, and he contributes greatly to its great growth. He not only serves as the youth pastor but also directs a large music ministry. As his responsibilities would indicate, he is a very busy person. However, as you read this book, you will immediately recognize that his total dedication to his family is his first priority, as far as human relationships are concerned. He is the husband of a beautiful and dedicated wife, Dana, and he is the father of three wonderful children. In addition to these many time-consuming activities, he is constantly involved in counseling and encouraging young people.

Regardless of your age, you will find *Life Quest* a very interesting read. I found myself contemplating how I could help the age group that the book confronts. However, the longer I read, the more I realized that much of what is taught in this book is very helpful to all of us. I not only enjoyed this book (by the way, enjoyed is the right word—I found myself laughing at times and crying at other times), but I also profited from the wonderful principles and precepts found throughout the book.

I am thrilled that Cary has disciplined himself and is regularly writing books that are making a great impact. This is a must-read for every young adult and a very useful resource for all who are concerned about and desire to help young adults.

I am delighted that I have had the opportunity to be involved in ministry along with Cary. He has been a great source of encouragement to me, and he is a very joyful man. His attitude exuberates joy. I am honored to call him my friend, and it is a great honor for me to be able to recommend this book to you.

# From the Author

Dear Reader,

The book you hold in your hands is meant to compel you forward in life. Increasingly, our culture is dumbing down and holding back young adults. Young adults are choosing not to grow up. Out of fear, frustration, or pure folly, they are choosing to remain dependent upon parents and teen-ish in their thinking well into their thirties. This isn't merely a social problem, as most sociologists and developmental psychologists believe. It is a spiritual problem. Young adults of this culture are paying a high price to remain immature, and they won't know it until it's much too late to do anything about it.

The changes of culture aside, God calls us forward in life. He calls us to maturity and responsibility. Culture calls us to folly and frivolity. Societal pressures, cultural philosophies, and personal folly must be set aside, and you must embrace a bigger prize.

In these pages, you will discover the huge rewards of biblical, passionate adulthood. If you go with culture, you're missing out! If you go with God, you win.

These pages address a societal problem that is prevalent and well documented by secular psychology and sociology. Yet, these secular professionals fail to see or understand the spiritual causes and the biblical cures. They merely observe and wonder what it means and where it will take us.

This problem, however, is not new to God. Two thousand years ago, Jesus told the story of the prodigal son, and thousands of years before that, Cain killed his own brother when he was yet a young adult. Young people have been ruining their lives for a long time. God has answers for emerging adults, and these pages will point you to them!

Thank you for taking time to read. May the pages to follow challenge you to grow in God's grace and to embrace life passionately in His purpose.

Sincerely,

Cary Schmidt
Associate Pastor
Lancaster Baptist Church, Lancaster, CA
November 2006

"[Young adults] don't think long-term…. They're concerned about their careers and immediate gratification."
—*Bill Frey, Demographer*
  *Brookings Institution*

"…They're not just looking for a job. They want something that's more like a calling, that's going to be an expression of their identity."

"This is a period of exploration, instability, possibility, self-focus, and a sustained sense of being in limbo."
—*Dr. Jeffrey Arnett, Developmental Psychologist*
  *Clarks University*

"There are joys and satisfactions that come with assuming adult responsibility. If those who are 30 and older want the rest of the world to grow up, they'll have to show the twixters that it's worth their while."
—*TIME Magazine*
  *January 2005*

"Eventually the future catches up with those who follow the philosophy of immediate gratification."
—*James Cote, Professor of Sociology*
  *University of Ontario*

"Many people are simply not growing up…. [They] emerge from a vague and prolonged youth into a vague and insecure adulthood. The transition to adulthood is becoming more hazardous, and the destination is becoming more difficult to reach if it is reached at all."
—*James Cote, Professor of Sociology*
  *University of Ontario*


"Most of the problems that twixters face are hard to see, and that makes it harder to help them."
"…There are few road maps in the popular culture—and to most twixters, this is the only culture—to get twixters where they need to go."
—*TIME Magazine*
  *January 2005*


"Their individualism makes them feel they have a responsibility to depart from their parents' religious teachings, no matter what those teachings were."
"…Most of them reject moral absolutes."
—*Dr. Jeffrey Arnett, Developmental Psychologist*
  *In a personal email dated October 18, 2006*


"[One young lady states] 'Everyone expects me to glide off smoothly into a good life, but I can't even see what a good life would be—let alone decide how to go about it.' … The long road to maturity exposes young people to grave anxieties."
—*Dr. Terri Apter, Social Psychologist*
  *Cambridge University*

"My sheep hear my voice, and I know them, and they follow me."
—*JESUS*
   *John 10:27*

"For I know the thoughts that I think toward you, saith the LORD, thoughts of peace, and not of evil, to give you an expected end."
—*GOD*
   *Jeremiah 29:11*

"...Fear not...I am thy shield, and thy exceeding great reward."
—*GOD*
   *To Abraham in Genesis 15:1*

"...speak unto the children of Israel, that they go forward."
—*GOD*
   *To Moses in Exodus 14:15*

"But they that wait upon the LORD shall renew their strength; they shall mount up with wings as eagles."
—*GOD*
   *Isaiah 40:31*

# Quest

*"an expedition made
by a knight to accomplish
a prescribed task
for his king."*

*The LORD is good
unto them that wait for him,
to the soul that seeketh him.*
—LAMENTATIONS 3:25

# SNAKES ON A PARKING LOT

*Escaping the Collective Cultural Coma*

Ever meet someone who loves snakes? Not normal. Something's wrong with these people. Somewhere, somehow they missed something essential in the gene pool. Personally, I hate snakes. It's not fear really. It's just that there's nothing to like about them. In my humble opinion, the only good snake is a dead snake.

In Milton, Florida, there's a park just on the north side of town that runs along the beautiful Blackwater River as it empties into the Escambia Bay. It's a quiet, peaceful place with picnic tables, shady spots, a boat launch, and one less snake than it had a few months ago.

We had just completed a few hours of boating with my parents. The boat was back on the trailer, the kids were in the car, and I was making one last trip to the trash can. That's when I happened across a baby snake slithering its way through the grass toward the parking lot. "Oh good," I thought, "another snake gets to die!" And I began planning his demise.

Should I step on him? Should I grab a stick and beat him? Should I pour gasoline on him and set him on fire? So many excellent choices! All the while, I'm watching him, following him toward the parking lot.

I knew exactly where he was headed. He was on the river side of the parking lot and was planning to go across the lot (about twenty-five yards) and into the woods. He was determined to get there. This was a snake on a mission— but he was completely unprepared for what he was about to face.

By now my family, waiting in the car, was wondering why I was mesmerized with the ground, but I was in no hurry, and I couldn't take my eyes off him. I couldn't let him get away.

Then, the coolest thing happened. He reached the pavement. Now, this was one hot summer day in the middle of a heat-wave, and the pavement was at least 110 degrees. First ten yards, he was fine, and I was tracking closely behind. Next five yards, I noticed he slowed slightly. I was puzzled. The next five yards he really began to struggle and couldn't go much further. Finally about one yard from the pavement's edge, the sun set on his young life. He was toast—literally!

I never touched him. He never saw me. I never intervened. He just cooked himself. It was awesome! I just love watching snakes die.

I've seen a lot of young adults start out the same way, and so have you. Many begin their quest into adult life with some grand destination in mind, some incredible dreams to realize, only to find out they were ill-prepared for the journey before them. They launch out into life self-confident, self-assured, and self-centered only to cook themselves into trouble before youth is even out of sight.

That little snake never knew what happened. He had no clue what he was up against and how ill-prepared he was to face it. And so goes the lives of many young adults in the twenty-first century. Crash and burn and then spend the rest of your life picking up the pieces. That seems to unwittingly be the life motto of many people in their twenties today.

Your story isn't all that different from that little snake's. The roles are somewhat reversed. Rather than being a snake stalked by a person, you are a person being stalked by a snake. He is definitely planning your demise, but he would be just as content to stand by and watch you cook yourself!

> *Childhood must become a memory and the future must be pursued by God's grace.*

You spent your early years by the river's edge where the grass was lush and life was easy. Somewhere across the hot pavement of young adulthood you envision your dreams and desires all becoming reality. It's getting from here to there that's confusing, scary, frustrating, discouraging, and sometimes seems not worth the effort.

Some young adults charge ahead, unprepared and ignorant, and they seem to do just fine for the first twenty or thirty yards. Cooking yourself takes time. Sometimes you don't even realize what you've done until it's too late.

Most young adults in today's culture are deciding that the journey across the pavement into the future just isn't worth it. They've watched too many people before them crash and burn. They let fear cripple them, comfort woo them, and irresponsibility allure them. The river's edge seems like a nice place to spend the rest of your life. Why grow up if you don't have to? Why not prolong this Neverland existence into your twenties and thirties? It sure beats cooking on hot pavement.

Others take a different approach entirely. They realize that childhood must become a memory and the future must be pursued by God's grace. They understand that He is a God of purpose, direction, and forward motion. He invites us to diligently seek Him, and He promises to reward us when we do. They realize that life must move forward. And rather than freeze in fear or frustration, they take a different path across the hot pavement. They choose to pursue those dreams, that future, that purpose in the will of God. They choose to diligently seek a future that looks so promising yet so far away.

And hence we arrive at the central message of this book—getting from here to there. Choosing to adventure forward in a culture that's moving backward. Choosing to embrace adult responsibility, adult challenges, adult decisions and then enjoying the immense blessings that follow. Choosing to believe that growing up and seizing the future is worth the risk, the effort, and the pressure. I almost called this book "Grow Up—It's Worth It!"

Sure, growing up is sometimes a pain. Sure, everybody who grows up eventually dies. Sure, the pavement is hot sometimes. But growing up is worth it! Facing your future courageously in the will of God is worth it. Leaving Neverland is worth it. You may not believe me now, but hopefully by the end of this book you will.

In January of 2005, TIME magazine featured a cover story that profiled a new phenomenon in American culture. The story was entitled "Meet the Twixters," and it detailed the cultural evolution of a new age-group—a generation that is refusing to grow up. If you are between seventeen and thirty, you are a part of that generation.

*Facing your future courageously in the will of God is worth it.*

The article described what I would call a "collective cultural coma." It detailed how young adults are attempting to hit the pause button on life somewhere between twenty and thirty years of age. They are refusing to accept adult responsibilities and rejecting the idea that they must move forward from their childhood and teenage years. This is not a passing fad affecting merely some of this generation, but rather a new trend reflected throughout culture.

Let me share some excerpts of this disturbing article and the trend it exposes. Stay with me; this all has a point!

The author states that these young adults "live off their parents, bounce from job to job and hop from mate to mate...having fun but seemingly going nowhere. This is a generational hiccup."

"Social scientists are starting to realize that a permanent shift has taken place in the way we live our lives. In the past, people moved from childhood to adolescence and from adolescence to adulthood, but today there is a new, intermediate phase along the way. The years from eighteen until twenty five and even beyond have become a distinct and separate life state, a strange, transitional never-never land between adolescence and adulthood in which people stall for a few extra years, putting off the iron cage of adult responsibility that constantly threatens to crash down on them. They're betwixt and between. You could call them twixters."

The article continues: "This new period is a chance for young people to savor the pleasures of irresponsibility. ... researchers fear that whatever cultural machinery used to turn kids into grown-ups has broken down, that society no longer provides young people with the moral backbone and the financial wherewithal to take their rightful places in the adult world. Could growing up be harder than it used to be?"

Later the author describes: "...parents were baffled when their expensively educated, otherwise well-adjusted 23-year-old children wound up sobbing in their old bedrooms, paralyzed by indecision. Legally they're adults, but they're on the threshold, the doorway to adulthood, and they're not going through it."

Perhaps, as a young adult, you can identify with these feelings. You may find yourself trapped in the middle of this messed-up mindset—this collective cultural coma—brought on by a generation gone before you that has collectively dropped the baton. We've reared you on video games and TV shows like "Friends," leaving you completely unprepared for your future. For your generation, life is about high-scores and sleeping around between parties and visits to coffee shops.

Yes, my generation has failed you. It's no wonder you don't want to grow up. We've taken away all reason and ability, leaving you with empty dreams and a complete lack of motivation to seize the future. Consider this:

1. *We've taken away your God.* We've kicked Him out of school, taken His laws away from your heart, told you He doesn't exist, and refused to let you pray to Him in public. Therefore you have no purpose for existence, no hope for eternity, and only death to look forward to. Without Him, life doesn't mean anything, and there are no absolutes upon which to stake your future.

2. *We've told you that you evolved from nothing.* The only option when you destroy the Creator is to try to convince you (against mountains of indisputable evidence) that you came from nothing and that you mean nothing. We've taught you in public schools that you are merely random biological matter that is evolving into something else. Your existence is purely accidental, and life is merely a survival of the fittest. So, if we're just animals, why should you care to grow up—it really doesn't matter, if evolution is king!

3. *We've shown you horrific examples of marriage and family.* In record numbers, our marriages have fallen apart. No one knows this better than you. Chances are better than fifty percent that you experienced this firsthand, growing up with a single parent or a step-parent. If you take our generation's statistics

by themselves, you would have to conclude that marriage doesn't work and that it's not worth trying. If you've grown up with a mom and dad together, you are most blessed, and if they are happily married, well congratulations—that's all but extinct in this culture! As a whole, we haven't given you much reason to look forward to marriage and family.

4. **We've taught you that sex can be with anyone at any time for any reason—safely.** What a lie! Again, this is the only logical conclusion if God doesn't exist, evolution is true, and marriage doesn't work. This deadly lie is cooking more hearts and souls than I can possibly describe in one book. You don't realize you're being cooked by this one until you're nearly well-done, flat on the pavement, barely aware of what hit you. This one is big. Really big. We'll come back to it later in the book.

5. **We've become disillusioned with our jobs and careers.** Over thirty percent of working adults (including your parents) hate their jobs. They trudge through commutes and daily chaos like walking zombies, hardly inspiring you to go and do likewise. They thank God for Fridays and despise Mondays. They play on three-day weekends like there's no tomorrow. Generally speaking, their lives are empty and pointless. Work, pay bills, sleep, eat, work, pay bills, sleep, eat—over and over in hypnotic redundancy. We haven't given you any reason to want this life, much less pursue it!

6. **We've taught you that life is about fun.** Though we have to work to provide for your life, we've tried to provide fun. In fact, as parents and adults going before you, we've swallowed the lie that the more fun we can provide for you, the better job we're doing!

We say things like, "You'll have the rest of your life to work; have fun while you're young." We've filled your life with iPods, ESPN, entertainment, and video games. We've taught you that this is the stuff of "real living"! We've sadly misled you. We'll visit this in another chapter.

7. **We've taught you to take the path of least resistance.** Like no generation before you, we've tried to create the easiest path possible for you. We've tried to remove every discomfort and give you every pleasure. We've taught you that life is about being comfortable and having pleasure. We've taught you to avoid anything that requires more of you than a remote control would.

These things have created a collective cultural coma. The TV, the music, the mass media, the video games have desensitized your generation and drained you of life and reason to live. Most young adults in their twenties are mere shadows of who they really should be by God's design—but they're incredibly accomplished on PlayStation, and what a difference it has made in the world!

Your generation has morphed and mutated a sort of prolonged, never-ending adolescence—a new and improved version. You're older than a teenager, smarter than a teenager, and have more freedom than a teenager, but no additional responsibility and no higher cost. All the gain minus the pain! What a deal—or so it seems on the surface. We'll find out otherwise.

And so, your generation is weak, feeble, and passive.

We have dropped the baton of adulthood. We haven't prepared you. In fact, we've robbed you of some very important information and some very enjoyable blessings. We missed it, and so we've misled you as well. We rejected God, and now we've left you hopeless. We've scared you *motionless.* We've taken away every reason you should have for pressing forward courageously.

Please don't feel that I'm insulting you. If you don't fit this mold, God bless you! You are in the vast minority for your generation. But even so, there is a great chance that you identify in some way with the portrait that I'm painting. For the most part, even Christian young adults experience this coma.

I have a friend named Joe. He became a Christian in tenth grade, and I've watched him grow into a fine young man with a heart to serve God. The thing I like about Joe is that he just speaks his mind. You never know what he might say, but he's just honest. Not long ago, as he was boarding a plane to a new teaching job in a distant state, his simple words to me were these:

"Life is scary! I mean, yeah, it's exciting and all, but man I'm scared! In a little while I'll be getting on a plane to I don't know where...and it seems risky...it's scary!"

Another young man recently said to me, "Life is just easier if you don't care about anything."

The path of least resistance—I have to tell you, it's a sham. It's not all that it's cracked up to be. There's a better way. Life is worth living on purpose for a purpose. There's a way to get safely from here to there and even enjoy the journey!

Yes, growing up is *worth it*.

Last week, my wife and I sat down with our three children to play the Game of Life. For two hours we turned the spinner, moved our little cars, picked our careers, spent our money, added little pink and blue people to our families, and raced to retirement! It all seemed so simplistic. Worse yet, it all seemed so random—like all of life was based on the ever-sovereign spinner!

My oldest son Lance spun, and BOOM, "you just had a baby girl!" My daughter spun, and WHAM, "you just got married!" I spun, and WHACK, I have to pay forty-five thousand in taxes! My wife spun, and SURPRISE, "you're now a doctor!"

At the end, we all ended up at the same place—Happy Acres and Millionaire Estates—retirement-ville. Some arrived before others, but we all eventually got there. Then to find the winner, we counted our money.

That's when it hit me. This generation believes that life really is played that way! We live like it's all a random game, as if fate has some gigantic spinner recklessly moving us forward through time. The goal is to have as much fun and get as much money as you can. And in the end we all end up dying. It's all just some strange game.

So what's the point? Why try? Why waste your time caring about life if it doesn't matter?

Well, it *does* matter. There's a lot worth caring about. More importantly, there's a God who created you for a specific purpose. You matter. Your future matters, and it's worth pursuing.

In the coming chapters I would like to help you escape the coma and courageously embrace God's plan for your adult life. I would like to give you what my generation has failed to give you—a *reason* and a *route* to get from here to there.

God gives us a great promise if we will reject the cultural coma and choose to journey into life with Him as our refuge. He says, "A thousand shall fall at thy side, and ten thousand at thy right hand; but it shall not come nigh thee. Only with thine eyes shalt thou behold and see the reward of the wicked. Because thou hast made the LORD, which is my refuge, even the most High, thy habitation" (Psalm 91:7-9).

In other words, while most young adults are cooking themselves like snakes on a parking lot, your life can be different. You don't have to destroy your future before it really begins. You can take an entirely different course into adulthood—one of blessing, confidence, commitment, and integrity. Yours can be a life quest with no regrets.

As you read this book, we will journey together through three sections. I hope you will find a quiet place, grab a cup of coffee, open your heart, and allow the Lord to grow you through the principles we will study. Take your time, and let the truth sink deep into your heart.

In part one, we will discover five basic reasons why an entire culture of young adults is postponing adulthood as long as possible.

In part two, we will gain a small glimpse of what you will miss if you buy into this cultural slip-and-slide. We'll see three major reasons why your adult life will be worth pursuing *passionately*.

Finally, in part three, we'll talk about getting from here to there—successfully and enjoyably making the journey. We'll discover principles and character traits that will sustain you and strengthen you in your quest for the best life. And hopefully by the time you put this book down, you'll have an entirely different perspective on life than most of your generation.

I sure had fun watching that little snake die. I wonder what was going through his mind as his cooked little body gradually refused to move forward. Maybe he was thinking, "oops...." Maybe he thought, "Now I'm toast...." I don't know.

I could have helped him. I could have reached down, picked him up, and dropped him into the woods just a few feet away. But it was so much more fun watching him die!

Aren't you glad I'm not God? Fortunately, He gains no pleasure in watching you cook yourself on the pavement of young adulthood. He would much rather assist you on your

> *Your future matters, and it's worth pursuing.*

journey if you would allow Him, but you'll have to choose to move forward in a culture that is moving backward. It won't be easy, but it will be worth it.

Okay my friend, it's time to leave the safety of the riverbank. Scary? Maybe a little. Uncertain? Through your eyes—yes. Through God's—no. Difficult? Yes, but not so much that you can't handle it with God's help. Uncomfortable? Yes, at times something like a root canal. Unpredictable? Only for *you*. Not for *God*. It's time to move across the pavement and into that future that God has prepared you for—without cooking yourself.

Life is about to become a little hotter but ultimately a lot better! You'd better grab something a little more "heat resistant" for the journey. Let's find out how to get from here to there safely! Remember, it's worth it!

And do me one favor. If you feel bad for the little snake, go have your head examined.

*Happy is he that hath the God*
*of Jacob for his help, whose*
*hope is in the LORD his God.*

—PSALM 146:5

# PART ONE

# WHAT'S HOLDING
# US BACK?

*Root Causes of
Refusing to Grow Up*

# WHAT'S HOLDING US BACK?

*Like chains holding you hostage to childhood,
there are some primary reasons that your
generation is refusing to accept the call to
grow forward into adult life. Regardless of
how many you immediately identify with,
somehow these causes will work hard to keep
you from becoming who God made you to be.*

*Before you can understand how to successfully
and safely enjoy your young adult life, you
must honestly face what's holding you back.*

## CHAPTER ONE

# I WANT TO BE FOUR AGAIN

*Overcoming Immaturity and Irresponsibility*

I t was a beautiful spring Thursday afternoon. My
daughter Haylee had just come home from a half-day of
kindergarten, and I was enjoying a relaxing afternoon off.
The sun was shining, my wife and I had enjoyed a wonderful
breakfast out together, and life was good.

Suddenly, cutting the stillness like fingernails on a
chalkboard, Haylee came running into the living room
where I was, threw herself in an emotional collapse on the
couch and began sobbing like only a woman can. For a split
second I had an emotional vapor-lock—it's my day off, not
supposed to deal with problems on a day off, just supposed
to relax and be happy. It's then that I noticed her tearful
eyes peaking carefully above her moistened elbow (which
was wrapped around her face) to see if I was noticing her
suffering. That's when I realized that I was the reason for the
episode. Somehow, this was all about getting my attention,
or else she could have had her meltdown in any other room
of the house. No, she needed me to notice. By this time,

she was only getting louder and more dramatic, so I figured I'd better say something before she coughed up a tonsil or something.

"Haylee, what's wrong?" I played along with her game by sounding as genuinely concerned as possible. I knew by her tone that this was not a life-threatening issue. Believe me, she sounds completely different when something really deadly happens—like being attacked by a fly.

It was then that she blurted out, "I want to be four again!" barely getting the last word out before collapsing in another round of tears, moans, and drama.

"Why do you want to be four again?" I would soon wish I hadn't asked.

Collecting herself emotionally and blurting out quick statements between sobs and heaves, she began to list her grievances with being five years old: "Because every day (sob) I have to wake up early (sob, sob) really, really early (three sobs) and get ready for school! (breath, sob) Then I have to go to school and work! (heave, sob, breath) And work, and work, and work, and work...(another minor meltdown with multiple sobs and quick breaths) Then I have to work all day (sob) and get so tired (sob, sob) and I don't get to sleep in anymore (heave, sigh, sob) or watch Blue's Clues with Mommy or read books or play with my toys or have any fun! (another meltdown followed by long sobs) I just want to be four again so I can stay home and not have to go to school and work all day! (final meltdown...the point of no return)."

At this point, I joined her on the couch, sat down beside her, and being the stupid man that I am, I did my best to say something thoughtful and sensitive. The first thing that came to mind was...

"Haylee, if you're having such a tough time in kindergarten with only a *half day* of school, how in the world will you handle next year when you're in school *all day*?"

At that, she quietly moaned "I don't know" in long, drawn tones and collapsed in my arms. (Strike one for dad! Like I said, stupid man.)

Not good, I thought. Rewind and try to recover. Second attempt...

"Haylee," I said, this time holding her face in my hands and looking into her eyes, trying to sound as sensitive as I could, "you *have* to go to school, because if you don't you'll grow up to be stupid..." (strike two). The words were barely out of my mouth when I thought, what an idiot! I half expected Haylee

> *God has a purpose for these years that must be embraced.*

to sit up, stare me down and say, "You know, you're really not very good at this...."

Instead she responded again in tears, "Nuh, uh...I already know my letters and my numbers. I know how to read now. I already know everything I need to know. I just want to be four again." With this her inner hurricane had settled to a category one—minor whimpering.

Well, rather than strike out, at this point I just picked her up, put her in my lap, and held her. "Oh, you're going to be just fine. It will all work out, you'll see." She sighed, put her head against my chest, and just waited there for a long time, quietly enjoying Daddy's embrace. (Finally, the stupid man puts one out of the park! That's all she wanted to begin with. Be patient with us, ladies, we really are that stupid!)

As I look at your generation, I hear and see the same kind of heart cry, only it goes something like this: "I want to be twenty forever! The pressure of adult life, the weight of the decisions, the stress of the responsibilities are more than I want right now...."

On more than a few occasions, as a student ministries pastor for over fifteen years, I've had long heart-felt talks with spiritually paralyzed nineteen-year-olds. They sit in my office or across a table from me at a fast-food restaurant;

their eyes well up with tears, and they describe a new and confusing life for which they were not prepared. They feel overwhelmed, lonely, confused, lost, scared, and frustrated. They hide it well while attending classes, dates, game nights, sporting events, and church activities, but it hits hard when they pillow their head at night and stare into the dark. It sinks in and weighs heavily when they are by themselves.

One young man recently said to me, "When I turned eighteen and graduated from high school, it's as though God put my entire life in a box and began to shake it up. And He continued shaking it through my college years. Everything changed overnight and continued to change—my friends, my school, my family, my time, my jobs, everything. Only one thing remained constant—my God."

Regardless of your age or maturity, you can probably identify with Haylee's overwhelmed emotions, only on a much larger and more significant level! Transitioning into adulthood has never been easy for any generation, but yours has more choices, more challenges, and more information to assimilate than ever before. It can be depressingly overwhelming. The sheer magnitude of the choices facing you, the information hammering you, and the risk threatening you can make any young adult want to avoid it all!

While your generation is postponing adulthood and overstaying in the land of childhood, *you* can't afford to do this! Though it seems emotionally safer for the moment, the ultimate risk and loss is greater than you can see and understand. You won't realize what you've done until it's too late. You'll never be able to turn back time and recapture these years, and God has a purpose for these years that must be embraced.

Your generation is choosing immaturity over maturity—choosing irresponsibility over responsibility. It's easier. It's more fun. But it's the wrong choice. It prevents the future from unfolding the way God intends, and it morphs your life into a distorted mess. This mentality prevents your spiritual growth in ways that are indescribable. Sure, it's more convenient, less stressful, and more comfortable for the moment, but the price of these choices is high.

## Mature and Responsible—To Be or Not to Be?

It's strange, but you live in a world where young adults are more concerned with the kind of cell phone they have than the kind of character they are developing. They are more concerned with having fun than with finding purpose. They are wallowing in a pig-pen, playing in the mud of life, when they were created to feast at the King's table and live for His high calling! In short, they are choosing to stay *immature* and *irresponsible*.

How would you define maturity? Age? Status in life? Driving a car and working a job? What does maturity look like to you? This may shatter your pre-conceived ideas, but maturity quite simply is *the acceptance of responsibility*. Maturity shows up in a person's life not because they arrive at a certain age or status, but when they begin to truly own and accept the true, God-given responsibilities of life.

Now, if you're honest, you want people to see you as mature, and if you're like most, you believe that will be found in driving and dating. Culture tells you that if you work a job, drive a car, date other young adults, and dress a certain way—you are mature! Wrong. Way wrong!

Maturity isn't about squealing your tires and spiking your hair because "you're eighteen now!" Maturity is embracing life's responsibilities and accepting life's growing pains. Maturity can't be faked or put on; it must be deliberately chosen. Frankly, your generation is choosing to remain immature while demanding the privileges and pleasures that only maturity can have. They are choosing irresponsibility while expecting to be treated as responsible adults.

The Apostle Paul wrote these words to infant Christians who were struggling in spiritual immaturity: "When I was a child, I spake as a child, I understood as a child, I thought as a child: but when I became a man, I put away childish things" (1 Corinthians 13:11). Solomon wrote, "Foolishness is bound in the heart of a child..." (Proverbs 22:15). In Ecclesiastes he referenced that "childhood and youth are vanity" (Ecclesiastes 11:10).

Each of these verses calls you forward in life, not backward. Each of these verses divides cleanly between childhood and adulthood. In fact, Ecclesiastes 11:10 begins with a direct call to the emotions you are facing as a young adult. God says, "Therefore remove sorrow from thy heart, and put away evil from thy flesh: for childhood and youth are vanity." In other words, turn from the sorrow and remorse of not wanting to grow up; turn away from the sins that destroy so many young hearts and see the vanity of this thinking. It's as if Solomon was seeing the same problems in his generation—young adults refusing to embrace adulthood.

What's the difference between maturity and immaturity? Consider the following and examine your own heart as a young adult. Five things come to mind as glaring differences between the mature and immature.

> 1. *Immaturity seeks fun, maturity seeks responsibility.*
> 2. *Immaturity seeks comfort, maturity seeks growth.*
> 3. *Immaturity seeks pleasure, maturity seeks purpose.*
> 4. *Immaturity seeks immediate gratification, maturity seeks long-term blessings.*
> 5. *Immaturity seeks sin, maturity seeks righteousness.*

*1. Immaturity seeks fun, maturity seeks responsibility.* While most kids live for fun and candy, mature adults make a slightly different choice. Fun doesn't completely go away;

it just can't dominate your life as when you were a child. This might be a bitter pill to swallow, but again, it's worth swallowing and we'll see why later. Hang in there.

Maturity seeks to own responsibility. With every new adult privilege comes a world of new responsibility. With driving a car comes the safety of yourself and others around you, as well as the care and maintenance of the car. With a job comes hard work, being on time, reporting to authority, taking a stand, and pleasing your boss. With sex comes marriage, commitment, care, concern, and children. With any big blessing comes big responsibility. Maturity sees the responsibility and embraces it. Your generation wants the privilege without the responsibility. Your generation wants the car without the care, the sex without the commitment, the money without the hard work, the sin without the consequences. I promise, this will bite you bad if you don't change it quick. Responsibility isn't bad. It's a part of living God's plan for your adult life. Don't run from it—*embrace it.*

**2. Immaturity seeks comfort, maturity seeks growth.** While kids think about sitting around playing with toys and video games, mature adults seek to invest their lives into things that pay back—things that contribute to life rather than drain it. Television, toys, video games, and most entertainment put nothing into you. These things amuse, but they don't infuse. They occupy your brain while draining it of strength and life—comfortable but also crippling.

Think how much smarter or well-prepared you would be if you could take half of all the time you've ever spent on TV and video games and use it to read or grow in some way. Now think how far behind you might be if those things have dominated your life for any length of time. Worse, think how much farther behind you will be if you don't change course for the next ten years!

Maturity seeks to grow, to improve, to increase. Maturity isn't all about comfort and carefree living. Maturity looks for the opportunity to grow.

**3. Immaturity seeks pleasure, maturity seeks purpose.**
To the immature, life is about feeling good. Now, there's nothing necessarily wrong with "feeling good"—but to the immature, this becomes life's pursuit. From one good feeling to the next, they live for pleasure. The scary thing about this is it's possible to feel good while you're dying!

*The best blessings of life are worth waiting for.*

Good feelings are not the substance of life. Living for God's purpose is the substance of life!

Mature adults come to grips with the fact that God created them for His purpose and they get to it—they seek it, discover it, prepare for it, pursue it. Like Nike says, they "just do it"! They don't vegetate through life; they purpose through life. They have a reason to wake up, a reason to live, a reason for heading the right direction, and their reasons have nothing to do with MTV or Paramount Pictures. Their reasons are founded in purpose.

**4. Immaturity seeks immediate gratification, maturity seeks long-term blessings.** This is huge. Your culture is shouting, "Have it and have it now!" Whatever "it" is, there's no reason you can't just have it. After all, it's your life and you're a legal adult. Want sex? Go have it. It's free, it's easy to find, it's even "safe"—just go for it. (And if you happen to get pregnant, just kill it.) Want fun? Go get it, charge it, do whatever you have to do, just get it while you're young. Want to escape from life? Get drunk, smoke weed, live it up...for tomorrow you will be old and everyone knows that old people (anyone over thirty-five) don't have any fun. Want money? Don't work for it. Don't start at the bottom and work hard. Don't even bother learning a career. There are fast, easy, irresponsible ways to make lots of money now!

Your friends are buying these lies faster than they can be produced! Immediate gratification is a major let down. Don't believe me? Just look around; talk to a few people who will speak honestly about their diseases, their addictions, their abortions, their divorces, their pain, their emptiness, their emotional scars. Need I say more? This list could be much longer. You'll find that the allure of immediate gratification is a trap from which few recover.

The mature see life's pleasures and blessings in a completely different light. They know that the best blessings of life are worth waiting for. They understand that the pleasure of sexual fulfillment requires the patient discovery of a lifetime companion and true commitment in marriage. And they choose to patiently pursue the long-term blessing over the immediate gratification. They know it's worth the wait! The mature see money and financial stability as a long-term, patient pursuit that will require years of steadfastness, and they believe it's worth the wait. They see the big picture, and they know that choosing the long-term blessings will pay off big time eventually!

**5. Immaturity seeks sin, maturity seeks righteousness.** God says of Moses, "Choosing rather to suffer affliction with the people of God, than to enjoy the pleasures of sin for a season" (Hebrews 11:25). Sin is attractive and it even provides pleasure, for a season. Immaturity can't see beyond the pleasure—it seeks and follows sin wherever it leads with no thought of the consequences. It asks, "How much can I do without getting caught or hurt?" And for a while, this life looks great! Christian young adults even reason, "My friends aren't living for Christ and they seem to be doing okay...." Which is like thinking, "That man who just jumped out of that airplane with no parachute seems to be doing just fine...I guess I will too!" It appears that total abandonment of all biblical wisdom leads to a lot of fun—parties, friends, new experiences. But eventually the trap snaps. Eventually the parachute-less man will go "splat." Sin isn't worth it.

I have a huge golden retriever named "Mac." For my boys and me, he's fairly well trained, but you should see *Mac* take my *daughter* for a walk! Yes, I said it right. In her case, it's the dog walking the child. She has no control whatsoever, though she thinks she does. He goes wherever he pleases and she hangs on for dear life. That's how immature people are with sin. It's taking them for a walk and in the end, they always end up asking, "How did I get into this terrible mess, and what do I have to do to fix it?"

Mature people, on the other hand, know that righteousness rewards. They know that God's blessings are better than sin's pleasures. They willfully reject sin and choose the path of righteousness. They see beyond the parachute-less free fall (though exhilarating it may be) and they choose not to go "splat"! Meanwhile the free-falling people mock them, ridicule them, and make fun of them for being so "stupid." (just before they go splat that is...)

Here's how God says it, "For the LORD knoweth the way of the righteous: but the way of the ungodly shall perish" (Psalm 1:6). Again in Psalm 5:12, "For thou, LORD, wilt bless the righteous; with favour wilt thou compass him as with a shield."

So grade yourself. Are you mature or immature? Are you accepting responsibility, seeking growth, pursuing purpose, waiting for long-term blessings, and willfully choosing righteousness? Or are you the parachute-less man enjoying your free fall? Better wake up! Adulthood is upon you and God is calling you to maturity. There's no need to go "splat," unless for some sick reason you just need to make a mess of your life.

God says of full-grown adults who were supposed to know Him and follow Him, "For my people is foolish, they have not known me; they are sottish children, and they have none understanding: they are wise to do evil, but to do good they have no knowledge" (Jeremiah 4:22). They are foolish. They are "sottish"—which means they are silly.

And in their silliness they know a lot about evil, but when it comes to real life they are just plain stupid.

Let me ask you a pointed question. Are you willing to go through life completely stupid about spiritual things just because you want to have a little fun now? God says, be stupid about sin and evil, but not about life. When it comes to life, be understanding. Be wise. Be enlightened. Know where you're going and why. "Brethren, be not children in understanding: howbeit in malice be ye children, but in understanding be men" (1 Corinthians 14:20).

As you leave (or have left) your teen years, God calls you forward, not backward. He calls you to maturity, not immaturity. He calls you to responsibility, not irresponsibility. He created life to move forward—each year building on the last, each experience preparing you for the next, each assignment training you for something greater, and each new blessing bringing new responsibility. It's the law of life. You can't defy and win. Defy it to your own demise. You will lose every time. You can't stay a child. You can't avoid mature adult life anymore than you can avoid breathing. If you try, you will regret it. Immaturity, when chosen willfully, always leads to emptiness, while maturity leads to fullness—abundant life.

Maturity is even *more fun* than immaturity. Many of the wonders and joys of childhood that young adults are so hesitant to let go of will resurface with great delight and blessedness in God's plan for your future. The transition is needful, but it isn't detrimental! You're not saying goodbye to all fun, all comfort, and all lightness. You're going to be

*Embrace maturity and look forward to God's plan.*

surprised how it will show back up in your adult life, and you'll be so glad you grew up!

Life is about growth. Jesus "increased in wisdom and stature, and in favour with God and man" (Luke 2:52). God promises to spend the rest of your life doing a good work in you, "Being confident of this very thing, that he which hath begun a good work in you will perform it until the day of Jesus Christ" (Philippians 1:6).

Are you willing to rise out of immaturity and embrace maturity?

Everyone faces the "I want to be four again" syndrome. Everyone faces his own version of immaturity. Every young adult wrestles with overwhelming emotions during early adulthood. Like Haylee, we want to throw ourselves on the couch in despair, give up hope, and spend the rest of our lives eating Twinkies and watching "Blue's Clues." What we really want is the loving embrace of a Heavenly Father to remind us that He is there and that everything is going to be okay.

Haylee started first grade the other day. She's in school 'til three, handling more work, and loving life. She made the transition. She matured. Oh, she still enjoys reading stories on Mommy's lap, but she's not wishing she were four again. She survived and so will you. Don't look back in immaturity and long for yesterday. Embrace maturity and look forward to God's plan. Life is about to get even better.

## CHAPTER TWO

# LIVE STUPID, DIE YOUNG

*Overcoming Ignorance and Rebellion*

"Trust me...."

Those were the words of Troy to his ten-year-old daughter Meagan as they stood on the edge of the Ocean Avenue Bridge in Lantana, Florida, in September of 2006. Hand in hand, they were looking down a fifteen-foot drop into an intra-coastal waterway.

They were on an evening bike ride, when Troy had the brainy idea of jumping off the bridge into the water to help his daughter get over her fear of heights. You would think this fear was a real topic of discussion among the family at the time. So dropping their bikes, they mounted the edge of the bridge, at which point Meagan said, "It's kind of high...."

Well, apparently Meagan decided to trust her father, because they both jumped—from fifteen feet into eighteen inches of water!

You'll be relieved to know that Meagan, amazingly, was unhurt. Troy, on the other hand, broke his leg. Never was a broken leg more deserved by a stupid adult. Helping her dad to the shore fifty feet away, Meagan then rode her bike home to tell Mom and to get help. After calling 911, the two met police and medical services back at the shore of Bicentennial Park where Troy and his broken leg were painfully waiting.

Interestingly, the media reported that Troy had been arrested two years earlier for child endangerment when he attempted to buy crack cocaine from an undercover police officer with his daughter in the car. I guess the ninety days in jail really helped him learn his lesson and move on to more responsible things like aggressive, psycho-therapy bridge-jumping.

The icing on the cake of this ridiculous story was Meagan's closing words, "I'm not afraid of heights...."

When I look at culture, I see my generation (Troy) taking your generation (Meagan) by the hand and leading you to the edge of a bridge and saying, "Trust me...." It's the blind leading the blind. It's the lost, foolish, and scornful leading the young, simple, and ignorant. We've jumped off the bridge of life and hurt ourselves, and we're telling you to trust us. It's as though we're saying, "Go ahead, forget marriage, have lots of safe sex; you'll be just fine. Go ahead, have fun, party hearty; you'll be just fine. Go ahead, spend ten or fifteen years wasting your young adult life goofing off and looking for the next thrill; you'll be just fine." And as we're pushing you forward into failure, we're broken and bleeding, crying for help ourselves!

For the most part, the lives we're exhibiting to you don't provide many "success stories" on a spiritual level. We haven't shown you "the right way." Our marriages, careers, and families are not generally all that admirable. Truthfully, my generation is just as ignorant and blind about truth, love, and life as your generation is.

## Look Who's Calling You Stupid

May I share a different perspective with you? There is another "breed" of people on this planet. They stay happily married for life. They grow more in love with every passing day of marriage. They raise their families upon truth, give themselves to the next generation, and strive to live wisely day by day. They don't sleep around, drink around, party, smoke, or engage in the pointless folly of culture. They don't follow the drumbeat of culture, but rather the voice of God. They live life by God's grace and for His purpose. They reject the notion that immediate gratification is the best philosophy of life. And in the end they enjoy huge rewards. These people are not hard to find—they stand out in culture. They are different—but *happily* so! I wouldn't have my life any other way! But this lifestyle is a far cry from the *typical* twenty-something young adult of this culture.

No matter where you are or how you have struggled, God will give you a second chance to be a part of this group! You still have time to experience His best in your future! God will meet your every need and exceed your greatest dreams, if you will give Him a chance.

A couple of years ago, God answered a long time prayer and gave me the opportunity to take my wife to Hawaii for five days. We spent those days on the secluded and romantic North Shore of Oahu walking the sand, watching the sunsets, seeing the island, and growing more in love. Before the trip, several friends who had been to Hawaii told us to be sure to go to a luau. Now, I had never been to a luau before, so I had no clue what I was attending. The dictionary defines *luau* as "a Hawaiian feast usually with music and entertainment." Great, I'm all for a feast with entertainment, provided that it does not displease the Lord in the process.

One hundred and forty dollars later, I'm enjoying some fresh pineapple and watching my wife have flowers braided into her hair. The sun was setting, the meal was being prepared (which, for the money, had better be *unbelievable*), and the park-like area on the water's edge was only beginning to fill with tourists for the evening.

Somewhere between the braiding of flowers and the spear-throwing game, I became thirsty and stopped at the restaurant area to grab a Diet Coke with lime. You can't beat a fresh piece of lime in a Diet Coke!

> *Most people expect young adults to be stupid and rebellious!*

When I ordered my Diet Coke, the waiter (about twenty-five years old) laughed out loud at me! I must admit, this had never happened to me, so I was taken back. Nerdski then dropped his jaw and gaped at me like I was suddenly growing another head! This guy wasn't all there to begin with, but now he really had me puzzled.

"What's wrong with that?" I asked somewhat baffled.

"Well, dude, it's a luau!" He laughed out loud again like he couldn't believe how stupid I was. Now others are starting to notice, and I'm fishing for a way out of this because, frankly, I don't know where it's going!

He continued, "Aren't you going to *drink*?! I mean, you're not going to spend all that money and not *drink* are you?"

Now it was sinking in. He was shocked that I wasn't asking for alcohol. Apparently, it's tradition to attend a luau and get drunk—news to me.

Now, honestly, at first there was this "back of my mind" temptation to be slightly embarrassed. But then, something snapped me back to reality. I realized I was looking "stupidity personified" straight in the face, and *he's* trying to make *me* feel stupid! So, thankfully God gave me the courage to put it back on him.

"No, actually, I don't drink. I'm a Christian, and I'm a pastor."

Eyes wide and jaw dropped, he could only say, "WOW! You mean, you've never had alcohol?"

"Nope, and I don't intend to," I said flatly.

"Well, do you smoke?"

By now I'm thinking, look, I just want my Diet Coke… "Nope, never have, never will."

I really thought his jaw couldn't drop any lower at this point, but it did. "WOW," he said in a long drawn out tone as he finally started to pour my Diet Coke, "that must take a lot of self-control and personal sacrifice. You're really missing out on a lot!"

That really irritated me, so I shot back pretty quickly, "Well, not really—if you think about it. Let's see, alcohol tastes horrible to begin with, so I don't have to deal with hating it. Secondly, it costs a lot of money, so I save a ton! Thirdly, it's addicting, so it doesn't hold me hostage. And fourthly, when I go out to dinner with my wife and wake up the next morning, I'm not puking my guts out on the bathroom floor, and I can remember what I did the night before! No, actually I'm doing all right!"

That one short-circuited him. He stopped, stared for a moment, sort of drooled a little on himself, and then said, "Uh…I never thought of it that way…I guess you're right." With that he handed me a Diet Coke, and we parted ways.

The world tries hard to make pure, sincere Christian young adults feel *stupid* and *weird*, when in actuality it's the other way around. I share this with you first to prepare you. You'd better expect people to treat you this way. Second, you need the right perspective on it. If you're living to please God and following His truth, *you're* not the stupid one.

We live in a generation of unbelievable spiritual ignorance and rebellion. It is not only accepted (by parents and adults all over the globe), it is *expected*! Most people *expect* young adults to be stupid and rebellious! Amazing! You probably never thought of this, but our adult generation is the first generation in the history of humanity that has carved out eighteen years (from twelve to thirty) for young adults to act like idiots—and we call it acceptable! This period of time and this cultural mentality is a historical precedent! It has never been this way before.

Frankly, it should be insulting to you. Many of those ahead of you in life actually *believe* that you are emotionally, mentally, and socially incapable of being adult-ish and coping with the realities of adult life. Obviously, this is not the truth, but if you accept it unchallenged, then it may as well be! If you buy this lie, *you're* the one who loses.

So, here's my challenge to you in this chapter. Don't buy the lie. Don't believe that you are *supposed* to be rebellious and ignorant. You might call it "being single and free—born to be wild—having fun while you're young and single." However you say it, most young adults are choosing willfully to be ignorant and rebellious, and most adults over forty expect it, endorse it, applaud it, and even try to mimic it!

If you buy this mentality, prepare for pain. Prepare to say goodbye to your dreams and heart's desires. Because, while promising you fun and fulfillment, this path only leads to disappointment and despair. Sure, there are points on the journey that might include a moment's pleasure, but the destination is destruction. Satan is only too happy to tickle and tease you with fun while he leads you across the hot pavement slowly basting you.

## How Ignorance and Rebellion Go Together

You might be wondering why I grouped these two words together in this chapter as one of the generational flaws holding young adults hostage. Quite simply, rebellion is merely an exaggerated form of stupidity. It's stupidity cubed! Stupid people are not always rebellious, but rebellious people always have truckloads (I'm talking gigantic helpings) of stupidity.

Sometimes people *ignorantly* live in opposition to God. They don't know Him, don't understand His truth, and aimlessly wander through life looking for purpose and hope. Others *willfully* choose to defy God and live in rebellion. They know His truth but choose to be their own god and live their own way. The first group is ignorant, the second is rebellious—utterly stupid by choice.

Young adults of this generation are plagued with both—ignorance *and* rebellion. Because we've taken away God and His truth from mainstream society, we've taken away the knowledge of the Bible and the foundation of wisdom. Even many Christian young people are biblically illiterate. Just put them to the test. You'll find out that most Christian young adults know more about the hottest CCM (Contemporary Christian Music) artist than they do about the Ten Commandments or the basic principles of the Christian life. Most know more about *secular* artists and Hollywood's newest releases than they do about why they were created.

In conjunction with this obvious ignorance, young adults in record numbers are choosing to walk away from God, from His Word, from church, and from right living. The world looks too good. The fun is too alluring. Throwing the hearts of their parents and pastor to the wind, they run recklessly and heedlessly into sin and vice. Some even relish the fact that they are "rebels"—like it's a badge of courage— like they don't understand that their kind are a dime a dozen! And then they work hard to flash their lifestyle in the face of younger siblings and old friends who are staying faithful. If it weren't so sad, the magnitude of the stupidity would be laughable!

Now let me get personal for a moment. This chapter is about you rejecting ignorance and rebellion. Where do you line up in the description I'm giving? Are you choosing to be willfully ignorant of God's truth? Are you ignoring His plan and His purpose for your life? Are you tuning out biblical preaching and teaching and ignoring the Word of God?

How about rebellion? Are you defying what you know to be right? Have you refused to let God be God? Are you following the pleasure and sin of culture heedlessly and recklessly in the name of fun? Are you doing your best to crush your parents' and pastor's hearts?

You'd better wake up to the ignorance—the outrageous stupidity that has gripped your heart. God's grace is extending a hand to you. Turn back while there is still time.

## The Four People-Types of Proverbs

The Bible is filled with passages that address these issues of ignorance and rebellion, but none so repeatedly and pointedly as Proverbs. The point of the book of Proverbs is to make stupid people wise and to give rebellious people a second chance before it's too late. This is a book written from a father to a son, and because the Bible is God's Word, Proverbs is also a book from your Heavenly Father to you!

Throughout the book, the father (Solomon) is pleading with the son (Rehoboam) to hear his words, receive his instruction, and give his heart to the teachings. This is a father on a mission. He has seen some things, made some mistakes, wrecked some lives. He has experienced the price of his own stupidity—his own ignorance and rebellion in many areas, and now he writes his son in pleading tones, hoping that he will avoid that same fate.

Early in chapter one he writes, "The fear of the LORD is the beginning of knowledge: but fools despise wisdom and instruction. My son, hear the instruction of thy father, and forsake not the law of thy mother" (Proverbs 1:7-8). In other words, knowledge (the opposite of ignorance) begins with God! "My son, please hear my instruction and don't forsake it!" Can you hear his passionate panic? Can you feel his fervent fear for his son? Can you feel mine as I write this? Please, my friend, turn away from the ignorance and rebellion that is so popular and accepted in your culture and flee back to the Lord and His plan for your life! Please.

Throughout the book of Proverbs, Solomon repeatedly describes four kinds of people on this planet. He constantly contrasts the way they think, the way they live, and the end that they will find. He begs his son to see his life with the destination in view—to see the end from the beginning, and to live from that perspective. He warns of the danger of the wrong path and expounds the blessings of the right path.

You too will be surrounded by these four kinds of people. They personify the message of this chapter. You are one of them yourself. What are these four people-types?

> 1.   *The wise*
> 2.   *The simple*
> 3.   *The fool*
> 4.   *The scorner*

Let's look at them briefly. Honestly ask the Lord to show you which category you fit into right now. By the way, if you're in a category other than the wise, you don't have to stay there.

## The Wise

Proverbs also refers to this person as prudent, understanding, discerning, upright, good, and righteous. These are the good guys. This is what Solomon is praying and hoping that his son will become. It's what I'm praying *you* will become.

"A wise man will hear, and will increase learning; and a man of understanding shall attain unto wise counsels" (Proverbs 1:5). "Give instruction to a wise man, and he will be yet wiser: teach a just man, and he will increase in learning" (Proverbs 9:9). "The heart of the prudent getteth knowledge; and the ear of the wise seeketh knowledge" (Proverbs 18:15).

Page limits prevent us from examining the dozens of references to this kind of person in Proverbs alone. These guys have the best life, by far—hands down—no comparison! Just read for yourself. Do a simple survey of a few chapters of Proverbs. Richie Rich, Bill Gates, and all the lottery winners in history never had it this good. God takes care of these people because they honor Him. These guys have God's blessing, solid direction, keen insight, and quick discernment. They have an enormous advantage over the other three people groups because they "get it." They see things that these other groups completely miss. They understand. They know.

To the other three people groups, these guys are just really, really, really lucky. In fact, they say it that way! "Wow, you're so lucky!" It's not luck. It's the *path of righteousness*. It's the road less traveled—the path of most resistance. It's the high road, the safe route, the narrow path. It's doing what is right because it's right, and it aligns your life on a collision course with God's best blessings.

The good news—this is not an exclusive group of naturally gifted, upper-class preppies. No, anyone can be in this group. In fact, anyone from any life stage or social class can be in any one of these four groups. These descriptions are about heart quality and core character—not about social status or family income.

How do you get into this group? By asking. God clearly says, "If any of you lack wisdom, let him ask of God, that giveth to all men liberally, and upbraideth not; and it shall be given him" (James 1:5). If you ask, you can have this wisdom. If you receive instruction, hear God's Word, and accept His truth, you can have this life.

## The Simple

This second group, believe it or not, is the closest to becoming the first group. The word *simple* means "silly or easily seduced." Proverbs also refers to this group as "void of understanding." These are the guys who don't "get it," but they would like to! They are utterly ignorant and just don't know it. It's not that they have a bad spirit, a wrong attitude, or a corrupt heart. They don't hate God or His Word. They aren't necessarily lazy, bitter, rebellious, or defiant. They are followers. They become like the people they are with.

They have the potential to become wise, "O ye simple, understand wisdom: and, ye fools, be ye of an understanding heart" (Proverbs 8:5). Yet, they are blinded by ignorance. It's not blatant, willful ignorance like the next two groups. It's just plain ignorance. These guys believe everything that the fool and the scorner say—"The simple believeth every word: but the prudent man looketh well to his going" (Proverbs 14:15). And they totally miss the tell-tale signs of spiritual danger—"A prudent man foreseeth the evil, and hideth himself: but the simple pass on, and are punished" (Proverbs 22:3).

These are the guys who tie their shoes directly in front of a door that's about to open towards them. They think fast-food drive-thru jobs are long-term careers. They befriend whoever embraces them, follow whoever influences them, trust whoever talks to them, and they don't think any further than the end of their noses. Life is always about right now.

These guys are usually nice, but they should be locked up until they wise up. They are a danger to themselves. They don't think. They just laugh—whenever, wherever, about whatever. The Gomer Pyles of the world, they don't mean any harm, but if stupid were explosive, they would never make it through airport security.

The good news is, if you're in this group, you don't have to stay there. That's why I'm writing this chapter. That's why Solomon wrote Proverbs—"To give subtilty to the simple, to the young man knowledge and discretion" (Proverbs 1:4). "When the scorner is punished, the simple is made wise: and when the wise is instructed, he receiveth knowledge" (Proverbs 21:11). So, if you are still getting over your headache from tying your shoes in the wrong place or if you just found out that your french-frying abilities are not to be considered a vocation, then I have good news for you. You can be made wise!

Though simplicity is not limited to the young, it is definitely a part of youth—"And beheld among the simple ones, I discerned among the youths, a young man void of understanding" (Proverbs 7:7). My point is, there's no need to pretend that you don't have *some* simplicity still bottled up in you, no matter your age. If you're young, you're cursed with at least a little bit of simplicity. The sooner you accept this, the sooner you can be made wise. It's not that you're genetically stupid; it's just that you haven't lived long enough to accumulate the wisdom that God desires to give you over time.

I know many young people who came to terms with this somewhere around junior high, and they have long since taken the road to becoming wise. I know many clueless adults who radiate simplicity like the mid-afternoon sun on a cloudless day. They are way overdue on the wisdom timeline.

The simple could go either way—they could become wise or they could become fools. So, pursue wisdom! Like a starving refugee at a buffet, like a kid in a candy store—get wisdom and get understanding. Start asking, start listening, start receiving. You can't afford to stay simple, and you can't afford to get worse.

## The Fool

Group three is yet another step away from the wise. The root meaning of the word *fool* is "silly in a perverse way."

The word *wicked* in Proverbs can apply to both of these last groups. You might say that a fool takes simplicity to new heights of accomplishment and sinfulness. A fool gets serious about simplicity and turns it into perversion. A fool is more malicious, deliberate, and willful about sin and folly. He is savvier about his direction in life and more intentional about choosing sin.

These guys are bad in a silly, lazy, sinful, sleazy, and childish kind of way. They always think sin is funny, and they avoid all seriousness and responsibility in life. Like the simple, they love to laugh at wrong. They love to turn something pure into something perverted. They deliberately follow after sin, and they fully immerse their hearts in folly.

These guys talk wrong—"He that hideth hatred with lying lips, and he that uttereth a slander, is a fool" (Proverbs 10:18). They relish wrong—"It is as sport to a fool to do mischief: but a man of understanding hath wisdom" (Proverbs 10:23). They flaunt their sin—"Every prudent man dealeth with knowledge: but a fool layeth open his folly" (Proverbs 13:16). They don't believe that sin is wrong, and they don't believe that it will destroy them—"A wise man feareth, and departeth from evil: but the fool rageth, and is confident" (Proverbs 14:16). Worse yet, they won't listen to people who love them—"A fool despiseth his father's instruction: but he that regardeth reproof is prudent" (Proverbs 15:5). And when they are punished, it doesn't do any good—"A reproof entereth more into a wise man than an hundred stripes into a fool" (Proverbs 17:10). "As a dog returneth to his vomit, so a fool returneth to his folly" (Proverbs 26:11).

The sad news—there's little hope for this guy—"Though thou shouldest bray a fool in a mortar among wheat with a pestle, yet will not his foolishness depart from him" (Proverbs 27:22). The word *bray* means "to pound"! In other words, you can give a fool a serious pounding, and he's still a fool. These guys don't realize how close they are at all times to death—"...neither be thou foolish: why shouldest thou die before thy time?" (Ecclesiastes 7:17). Rarely do they become wise, and rarely do they live long—"...destruction shall be to the workers of iniquity" (Proverbs 21:15).

The good news is you're most likely not a fool, unless someone is *requiring* you to read this book. A fool would most likely never pick this book up, much less read this far. And God's instruction to you regarding fools? Here it is—"Forsake the foolish, and live; and go in the way of understanding" (Proverbs 9:6).

Finally, on this point, the *great* news: if a fool lives long enough, he will always end up subservient to the wise— "...the fool shall be servant to the wise of heart" (Proverbs 11:29). If you become wise, you'll probably end up hiring a few of these guys to do your grunt work somewhere in the future. They will just think you are *lucky*!

## The Scorner

This fourth group is the worst. The word *scorner* literally means "one who openly scoffs, derides, or mocks." Interestingly, the word also carries the connotation of one who is an ambassador, an interpreter, a teacher or one who intercedes. So think about that. This is a guy who openly scoffs and mocks God and righteousness, but he doesn't stop there! This guy takes it a step further. He's a teacher, an ambassador, an interpreter. He is on a mission. He's a *representative* of evil. By his own choice, he sides against God and tries to *recruit* others to do the same. He boldly and defiantly takes his stand against God and righteousness, and he unashamedly mocks Him. And he's out to take as many with him as he can!

While these guys come in varying degrees, they are bad—really bad. Usually, they are very angry. Their anger is probably rooted in some hurt in their past. Bitterness has become a stronghold in their spirit, causing venomous and willfully vile behavior. They truly hate God and blatantly resist Him. Their music, their friends, their internet usage, and their inner lives are usually influenced by satanic presences and demonic effects. Scorners are often found wearing black and are fixated with death and darkness. They are on a personal path of destruction, and they are taking others with them.

You can't rebuke them—"He that reproveth a scorner getteth to himself shame: and he that rebuketh a wicked man getteth himself a blot. Reprove not a scorner, lest he hate thee: rebuke a wise man, and he will love thee" (Proverbs 9:7–8).

These are the guys that avoid wise people altogether, and they prey on the simple and the foolish— "A scorner loveth not one that reproveth him: neither will he go unto the wise" (Proverbs 15:12). They are willfully, outwardly, flauntingly rebellious. They are recruiters, and they are aggressive about enlisting others to their scorn.

The Lord is very clear about handling these people. Though He loves them, they have rejected His love outright. Though He is merciful if they will turn back to Him, they angrily refuse His mercy. His hand of grace, they slap away. His heart of love, they spit upon. His offer of repentance, they laugh at.

So, He says, "Smite a scorner, and the simple will beware: and reprove one that hath understanding, and he will understand knowledge" (Proverbs 19:25). In other words, step one is to smite a scorner, not for the scorner's sake, but for the simple's. God commands authorities to punish the scorners so that others can learn and be spared—"When the scorner is punished, the simple is made wise: and when the wise is instructed, he receiveth knowledge" (Proverbs 21:11).

Then, God says, "Cast out the scorner, and contention shall go out; yea, strife and reproach shall cease" (Proverbs 22:10). When these guys are around, there is literally a satanic oppression of righteousness. There is strife and contention—deliberate resistance. These words refer to discord at a causative, root level. In other words, when you remove the scorner, you remove the cause of contention.

God's final thought in Proverbs about the scorner— "The thought of foolishness is sin: and the scorner is an abomination to men" (Proverbs 24:9). The word *abomination* is one of God's strongest words. A scornful spirit is among the most disgusting, repulsive things to His heart.

I'm fairly certain you're not a scorner unless you're reading this book in an effort to argue against it. But if you know a scorner, make no small effort to intervene in that life! Though it's rare, scorners can turn around by God's grace. (I've personally seen a few completely turn back to God.) Call on every biblical authority possible to rescue that scorner from the grip of anger and bitterness, but more importantly, protect *yourself* at all costs. Get away quickly and stay away. These guys are poison personified. You don't want to be influenced by them, and you don't want one person thinking you might be like them!

This chapter is about rejecting ignorance and rebellion, and embracing wisdom and understanding. The wise embrace adult life from a biblical perspective. The simple could go either way. The fool chooses to stay ignorant and laughs at it, while the scorner chooses rebellion and tries to enlist others to follow.

So, which person are you?

*The wise?*
*The simple?*
*The fool?*
*The scorner?*

Remember, you don't have to stay in the group you're in. You can move up the ladder. It's your choice...Now... Right now...And tomorrow, and the next day, and every day for the rest of your life. You will either be "becoming wise" or "becoming something else."

I'm so glad little Meagan didn't get hurt jumping off that bridge, aren't you? Nobody deserves a parent who would lead them to a fifteen foot jump into eighteen inches of water! Ironically, she ended up helping her dad out of a mess! Poetic justice at its finest! The young helping the foolish!

The point being, regardless of whether you have good parents or not, you don't have to make a mess of your life. Ignorance and rebellion don't have to lead you to jump! You already see the gaping wounds of a generation gone before you, but those wounds are the results of our own choices, not the result of God's failing us.

Friend, you don't have to live stupid and die young. God has a different plan for you. In fact, He will most likely use you to help someone older than you out of a mess! Poetic justice—you come and reach my generation with the Bible, the God, and the wisdom that we took away from you!

Refuse to be held hostage by ignorance and rebellion.

And for the record—we ended up sorely disappointed and leaving the luau early. If you ever go to Hawaii, take the $140 you might spend on a luau and go buy $130 worth of Q-tips and $10 worth of McDonald's value meals. Spend the evening flicking the Q-tips into trash cans several feet away and eating McDonald's burgers. You'll have more fun, the food will taste a lot better, and stupid drunk people won't annoy you!

## CHAPTER THREE

# A LESSON EVEN A DOG CAN LEARN

*Overcoming Folly*

G rowing up, my family had dogs. Going back to my first-grade year, I can remember a beautiful Siberian husky named Bandit. What a dog! She was big with a beautiful black and white coat and that super cool husky face that you've seen on sled dogs. Huskies are smart, expensive, "cut-above-regular" kind of dogs. There is only one problem that I have with huskies. As smart and cool as they are, they are super-stupid in one pretty important area. They love to run. Now that's not *why* they are stupid. They are stupid because they don't intuitively know *when* and *where* to run. (Or maybe it's that humans are stupid for trying to make them house pets when they really want to be sled dogs.)

I won't bore you by reopening my emotional wounds and revisiting all the scars. Suffice to say, these huskies gave me my first good series of heartbreaks. They are born to run and run they did.

It started with Bandit as we were moving from Alabama to Georgia mid-way through my second-grade year. She got out of the house on moving-in day and ran. Normally when she ran away, we could find her, though it usually took several hours and lots of effort. But on this particular day, she was in a new state, a new city, and a new street— and she just ran. Hours later—no Bandit. Days later—no Bandit. Many tears, phone calls, and anxious moments later, my mother finally found a vet who had a near-death, unclaimed husky that had been hit by a truck a few days before. Sure enough, that was Bandit, and sadly, she "passed on to glory" just moments before my mom arrived at the vet—heartbreak number one.

Being the great parents that they are, my mom and dad immediately set out to salve the young remorseful hearts of their three boys. They bought another husky. Her name was Panda—a slightly lighter, sleeker, and more stylish version of her predecessor. Panda was a really great dog. We even trained her not to run away, and when we moved again, we bought a house on five acres of woods in North Georgia where Panda could run to her heart's content. She always returned home because she loved us, and we fed her.

Only one problem—our house was surrounded on two sides by cow pastures owned by a cranky, coon-hunting, back-woods codger named Mr. Spruel. Now, Mr. Spruel wasn't the problem. Panda's love for *tormenting cows* was the problem. Panda had a habit of leaving the house, making a beeline to the cow pasture (about a quarter mile through the woods), and scaring Mr. Spruel's cows! They wouldn't give milk, wouldn't reproduce, wouldn't hardly even "moo" on key. Mr. Spruel didn't appreciate Panda. He and his greasy grandson even told us so on a few verbally colorful occasions. I distinctly remember the final threat being that he would shoot our "blank" dog if she did that again.

Shoot he did. Not dead, just paralyzed. My dad found her half-frozen in a creek bed halfway between our house and the cows—clean bullet hole through her spine. She was awake, whimpering, and completely immobile. I can still see that picture—him walking up the hill through the woods carrying Panda. That look on his face. I'm not sure if he felt bad for the dog or if he was pre-calculating the cost of the next dog.

A few hours later, at a vet down the road, Panda was lovingly sent to the great beyond. Back home, three boys were in tears again and Mom was trying to make us feel better—heartbreak number two.

A few days later, husky number three arrived at our home. (You know, the more I recall the story, I'm not sure who was dumber, the huskies for getting themselves killed, or us for buying more huskies!) We called her "Pepper." She was a lot like Panda but still "all puppy." Poor Pepper didn't have time to learn the ropes. She didn't even get to meet Mr. Spruel or his cows. Her life came to a quick end just a few days after her arrival when she bolted out the door at the first glimpse of freedom. There's just something irresistible about an open front door to the husky DNA. A few moments later, I caught up with her. Not because I was fast, but because a thoughtful motorist had intervened and used her car to stop her for me.

*Running from God isn't adventure or individualism —it's folly.*

I wrapped her up in my arms and carried her back home, blood dripping from her mouth, eyes barely showing signs of life. By this point, my sixth-grade heart was calloused enough not to feel too bad. After all this *was* number *three*! All I could think was, "stupid little dog…." I can't remember when Pepper died—just that she did. It was her own stupid fault. In fact, in every case, it was the dog's own fault.

It was about then that our family decided not to purchase another husky. Too wild. Too "needing-to-run."

Too self-destructive! You can't keep them alive long enough to love them.

Sounds like a lot of young adults I know. They're penned in, tied up, bound up by their own folly. They see the daylight of the world every time the door is opened. They salivate for it. They crave wildness. They long for what they call "freedom." They can't wait to run. The allure of the "great unknown" beckons them to run away and live the life they've always dreamed. They hate those who love them, despise that which protects them, and defy the God who created them. They can't wait to run. This isn't adventure or individualism—it's folly.

First chance they get—run they do! Fast and furious! Like the "simple become fools," they follow hard after the scorners who have recruited them. They fly fast—directly into the face of oncoming headlights—directly into the path of farmer Spruel's bullet. Taunting the cows was fun. Running from authority and from God was a *brief* but *bodacious* adventure. Fleeing restraint was glorious for all of a few moments—but it sure comes to a fast and brutal end every time.

Dr. Jeffrey Arnett, developmental psychologist from Clarks University, was kind enough to email me in response to my research for this book. In his email he made this statement of emerging adults, "Their individualism makes them feel they have a responsibility to depart from their parents' religious teachings, no matter what those teachings were." In a quest for individuality, they lose their individuality and become just like everyone else their age—running from reason! Regardless of truth, heedless of the obvious, they flee from God—the very *source* of their individuality to begin with, and they run to bondage!

Like those stupid dogs, these people are victims of their own silliness.

## Understanding Folly

There's a Bible word that often appears in the same verses with the words *simple* and *fool*. The word is *folly*. We saw it many times in the last chapter, but we didn't stop and talk much about it. The word sometimes means "silliness" and other times takes on a deeper meaning of "silliness in a morally wicked or perverse way." This is a sinful kind of silliness.

At best, this silliness is a worthless, passive distraction from something better or more godly. In other words, it might not be something overtly *sinful* as much as something *silly* that diverts you away from God's best. Remember when your parents or teachers would try to get you to focus on something more important by saying "stop being silly and listen"? It may not be that you were committing murder and mayhem; you just weren't giving your focus and heart to what really mattered.

At its worst, this word *folly* refers to something utterly destructive, morally wrong, and wicked. *Now* we're talking murder and mayhem. We might be talking immoral behavior, sexual sin, slime, and godlessness.

There's a lesson here. God uses one word to describe everything from minor distractions to major moral offenses. He calls it *folly*. Whether you're robbing banks, selling drugs, sleeping around, or just spending too much time in front of the TV, God puts it in the same category when it comes to life's purpose—it's all folly. It's silly. It's a waste of moments. It's the useless spending of life that diverts you from the purpose for which you were created.

Many young adults are snagged by folly. It comes in many shapes and sizes, but it boils down to the basic principle of wasting life. Take another look at these verses and give specific attention to this word *folly*.

"He shall die without instruction; and in the greatness of his folly he shall go astray" (Proverbs 5:23). Folly leads us astray from that which is right.

"Every prudent man dealeth with knowledge: but a fool layeth open his folly" (Proverbs 13:16). A fool often does not recognize the stupidity of his ways.

"The wisdom of the prudent is to understand his way: but the folly of fools is deceit" (Proverbs 14:8). Folly deceives a fool and blinds him to the truth.

"The crown of the wise is their riches: but the foolishness of fools is folly" (Proverbs 14:24). The life of a fool is summed up by this word *folly* or a fool's life is "utter silliness."

"Folly is joy to him that is destitute of wisdom: but a man of understanding walketh uprightly" (Proverbs 15:21). To the unwise, folly seems like a lot of fun.

"Let a bear robbed of her whelps meet a man, rather than a fool in his folly" (Proverbs 17:12). You'd be better off spending time with a very angry bear than with a fool and his folly. Hmmm...

"Answer not a fool according to his folly, lest thou also be like unto him" (Proverbs 26:4). Don't play a fool's game and dabble in his folly by debating it or responding to it!

"Answer a fool according to his folly, lest he be wise in his own conceit" (Proverbs 26:5). Biblically and wisely speak out and refute a fool's folly so the subtle danger is exposed.

"As a dog returneth to his vomit, so a fool returneth to his folly" (Proverbs 26:11). Though it's vile and repulsive, they just can't get enough of it.

"And I gave my heart to know wisdom, and to know madness and folly: I perceived that this also is vexation of spirit" (Ecclesiastes 1:17): When a man has all the folly his heart desires, it's like a disease of the soul, a vexation of spirit.

"Then I saw that wisdom excelleth folly, as far as light excelleth darkness" (Ecclesiastes 2:13). After exhaustively comparing wisdom and folly, Solomon came to the conclusion that wisdom was not even to be compared in its wonderfulness. Wisdom is everything that is right and folly is the opposite.

Folly—for the simple and the foolish is whatever leads him astray to destruction. It's the bait before the trap. In your case, it's whatever Satan must offer you or dangle in front of your face to get you to quit growing forward for God.

## Distraction Is Folly

Consider this question. What is most likely to get you off track spiritually? Mark it down—that's your folly. For most of us it's something different. For some it's sports. For others it's sexual impurity. For some it's a career dream. For some it's the god of education. For others it's friends. For some it's a hobby. For some it's a vice or addiction. For others it's a comic book or a game. Silliness. Diversion. A rabbit trail that leads off the road of purpose. Folly is anything that will help you throw ten years of life away while great decisions are left unmade—something that will distract you long enough to miss the greatest opportunities that God has prepared for you. Scary.

Folly is no laughing matter.

A few months ago, I gave my boys a Reuger 22 rifle. We live in a desert area, and there are a lot of places not far from our home where we can go shooting. More importantly, there are about forty million rabbits in this desert to shoot.

Not long ago, Larry and I went out to the desert to hunt some rabbits. This was our second time out hunting with the new gun and on this particular trip, the sun was setting quickly and we had missed a few rabbits. As the last rays of sunlight peeked over the mountains to the west, I told Larry we'd better head back to the car before we got lost in the dark.

A few steps later, I thought I saw a rabbit, so off we went. Sidetracked. Detoured. We were heading away from the car, hoping for that one last kill to tell mom about. At a little ridge I stopped, put the scope up to my eye and tried to discern if I was seeing a rabbit or not. Larry was just a couple feet in front of me and to my left.

Suddenly, piercing the silence like the most annoying baby-rattle you've ever heard, was a noise I didn't immediately discern. I was diverted by my own fixation with the rabbit. As if time slowed, I turned to look at Larry, almost asking, "What in the world are you doing?" As I did, he was looking down to his left and simultaneously backing up quickly. That's when I came to my senses and realized what the noise was.

*If you follow your desires, you're following a moving target.*

Rattlesnake!

This wasn't just any rattlesnake. It was a full-grown, Mojave Green rattlesnake—only the most potent and aggressive rattlesnake that God ever created. What a blessing!

He was about two feet from where Larry had been, coiled up tightly, head up, rattle blaring, ready to strike.

As you might guess, we freaked out—in a happy sort of way. At first we ran—five or ten steps in the opposite direction. Then we stopped, turned, and watched. Our hearts were pounding and adrenalin was rushing! He was still coiled, still rattling, still perturbed at us, but we had a gun. What a blessing!

About forty shots later, that snake was still moving. No head left, no rattle left, bullet holes riddling his body—still moving. Amazing.

Our hearts were pounding all the way back to the car—and you can bet we weren't looking for rabbits anymore! And WOW, did Mom appreciate that story!

Neither of us had any idea what kind of grave danger we were in just a few minutes prior to our rattlesnake encounter. We were too taken with our folly at the moment—finding and shooting rabbits! Yippee! To this day, I can't believe how stupid I was. I know that the desert is filled with rattlesnakes. I know they come out at dusk when the temperature cools down. I'm smarter than that. I know better than to do what we did. I should have been fully prepared for that experience. I should have seen that snake long before we were so close. Had that snake not had a rattle or had we taken another step in its direction, Larry would have surely been struck and probably wouldn't have survived long enough to get to the hospital.

A little folly sure can do a lot of damage.

The snake that's after you doesn't really care what your version of folly is. He just wants you distracted long enough to strike—long enough to destroy. Mark it down, folly is whatever takes your eyes off the trail of God's will and distracts you long enough to divert you.

What is your folly? How is the devil coming after you? Money? Fame? Career? Education? Lust? Anger? Friends? I'm sure you're thinking of it right now. Whatever it is, you'd better set it aside and choose to pursue God relentlessly. Folly is nothing to fool with.

In the final pages of this chapter, I'd like to highlight three major things that are "folly" to many young adults. There are many others, but these three find their way into the hearts of young adults more frequently. These are the issues I deal most with in counseling.

## Selfish Desires Are Folly

Danny and I sat in Panda Express, a fast-food Chinese restaurant near our church, when he asked a profound and deeply heart-searching question. I was proud of him for even asking.

"How can I keep from loving sports so much?" His eyes were searching and his heart sincere.

I knew what he was asking. I was looking at a young man who was unarguably the best athlete in our school at the time. He was good at everything he played. He truly loved sports. But somewhere along the way, God taught him that "sports" isn't a life's purpose. God didn't create people purely to play games. Games don't inherently fulfill God's eternal plan for the human race. He was awakening spiritually to the fact that God had a much broader and bigger plan for him, and he was beginning to see that his love for sports could threaten his heart for God.

Danny was seeing that sports could be folly.

In a moment of silent pleading, I asked the Lord for the right thing to say. What do you say to a young man to help him love sports less? That's when I saw the soy sauce packet sitting on the tray in front of me.

We were just finishing two big plates of great food— orange chicken, beef with broccoli, and lots of rice. I grabbed the soy sauce packet and held it up. I'm sure Danny wondered where this was going.

"Danny, sports is to life what this soy sauce is to this food we just ate. This isn't the main course—it's the flavoring. It's meant to be added to the main course to give it taste. No one comes into Panda Express and orders a plate of soy sauce. You order your main course, and you add the soy sauce as seasoning.

"Sports isn't the main course of life. Sports is the seasoning. Games are what you do on the side as you're living out your eternal purpose in God's plan. They give you a break, provide some exercise and fun, but they don't matter like living for God does."

Danny is still a great athlete, but he's a better Christian! He's in Bible college preparing to be a pastor. Something tells me that all the people he reaches, loves, and leads are going to be really glad he didn't go through life majoring on the soy sauce and missing the main course. They'll be glad he valued *them* more than *points!*

I know you have desires. And believe it or not, God is the Author of those desires, and He's going to fulfill them in ways you cannot comprehend. But we live in a world where selfish desires are king! We're taught to follow our hearts like they know where they're going! Ridiculous. Our hearts don't have a clue.

What you want today, you might not want next month. Desires change. Emotions ebb and flow. Dreams are the seasoning of life, not the main course. The "main course" of life is God's eternal purpose and glory!

Your dreams and desires will somehow play a part, but don't follow them, don't crown them king of your life, and don't worship them. Your grandparents might tell you to. Your friends might tell you to. Your teachers might tell you to. But don't listen to your heart. Listen to the Holy Spirit, the Word of God, and the voices of a multitude of godly counselors and authorities in your life.

Your desires will change. They will develop and grow. If you follow them, you're following a moving target that will forever lead you astray and never quite fulfill your heart. God is a fixed entity. He is your rock, your fortress, your refuge, your strong tower. He will never change, never let you down, never leave you, and never disappoint you. Your desires will. They will lead you to dead ends, get your hopes up and drop you hard, play with your emotions, and dangle imaginary carrots in front of your face. They don't care about you. Apart from God, they are folly!

Chasing your desires is like chasing rabbits in the desert. As soon as you see one, you see five more. They all run in different directions, and they change course repeatedly. It's impossible to keep up with them. You can't afford to spend your life running that kind of rat race trying to keep up with your emerging dreams and desires. They're just not trustworthy. God is!

Your Creator will not treat you so ridiculously. Cling to Him. Pursue Him. He is Almighty God, your loving, faithful Heavenly Father. Your desires? They are just figments of your imagination. Like vapors of steam floating off a boiling kettle, as soon as they appear they change shape and evaporate. They make really bad guides!

Don't let your desires become your folly. Let your God be King of your dreams, and watch over the next twenty years how He blows you away in fulfilling them!

## Fear Is Folly

The TIME magazine article I referenced in the introduction shares this quote: "In the past, people got married and got a job and had kids, but now there's a new ten years that people are using to try and find out what kind of life they want to lead. For a lot of people, the weight of all the possibility is overwhelming."

The author goes on to comment, "There was a time when people looked forward to taking on the mantle of adulthood. That time is past. Now our culture trains young people to fear it."

Did you get that? You're being taught by culture to fear adulthood. It is expected to overwhelm you. But you need to know—it's a set up. Culture is wrong. You shouldn't be overwhelmed by life the way God designed it.

Agreed, when you take God out of the picture, life is flat scary! Without Him, you have every reason to be paralyzed by fear. But with Him you have no reason to fear.

God's Word says to you in 2 Timothy 1:7, "For God hath not given us the spirit of fear; but of power, and of love, and of a sound mind." Courage is not the *absence* of fear, but rather faith to act *in spite* of fear! When facing big decisions you will experience fear, but you must realize this fear is *not from God* and you must press forward *through* it!

The Bible is filled with stories of young adults who faced overwhelming circumstances. Joseph was sold into slavery and cast into prison. Moses was called to lead a nation out of bondage. Joshua was called to lead the nation of Israel across the Jordan River into a series of wars. Rahab was compelled to help the spies at great risk to her own life. Gideon was commanded to take three hundred men into a battle against thousands. David was compelled to fight a giant against unbelievable odds. Peter was commissioned to preach the Gospel to first-century Israel. Paul was called to take the Gospel to the known world. Timothy was given the pastorate of one of the first churches in history.

These were watershed moments—pivotal circumstances in each young life where fear had to be confronted and defied. In every case there was great victory, great blessing, and great promise to be claimed. But in every case there was a mountain of fear and a young heart willing to climb it. And every time, fear was exposed as folly. God came through! He has never failed, and He won't *fail you!*

As a young adult, fear threatens to paralyze you in youthfulness, and culture tries to make you afraid. Yet, the more you understand the heart, the mind, the will, and the purpose of God, the less you have to fear. The more you walk with Him, the more He infuses your life with courage and confidence. The more you trust Him, the more you grow in faith.

While the world is trying to minimize risk and teach you to fear the future, you must recognize that there is no risk with God. When you belong to Him and pursue Him with your whole heart, He will lead and guide you. Every step is His leading and every circumstance His divine appointment.

The more you know God and trust Him with your future, the more you identify with Hebrews 13:6, "So that we may boldly say, The Lord is my helper, and I will not fear what man shall do unto me." No fear! No need to be terrified of what is to come. God promises a spirit of love and of power and of a sound mind. He promises to be your helper so that you have no need to fear!

What are you afraid of? What's keeping you from stepping forward? I know young adults who fear being on their own, fear committing to a relationship, fear getting a job, fear growing up. Without God, be very afraid. With Him, rest! There is no need to fear if you're following the Lord.

In God's economy, fear is folly.

"I sought the LORD, and he heard me, and delivered me from all my fears" (Psalm 34:4).

## Bitterness Is Folly

We have just one last stop on this road of folly. This one might surprise you.

A young lady came to me in tears, "My father hates me. He curses at me, calls me names, and threatens me. He tells me that he's kicking me out of the house as soon as I turn eighteen. He tells me how stupid I am, and it makes me feel worthless."

A young man came to me, "My father left when I was four. I've never known him. I've grown up with only one parent. My mom has done her best, but I don't feel ready for my future. I still want my dad."

Another young man came to me in tears, "My parents fight constantly. They yell, scream, throw things, curse, and threaten each other. Then, the anger comes out against me. I'm called names. I'm made fun of. I'm told how stupid I am. I don't know what to do, but I sure feel terrible."

A young lady broke down about the abuse her relatives put her through. A married man revealed how hurt he was over his wife's infidelity. A single young man was completely rejected and ridiculed by his parents for choosing to attend Bible college and serve the Lord. A single adult lady was coping with the lingering damage of a rape. An engaged couple was worried that they couldn't have a happy marriage because they had never seen one in their own homes. A young lady is betrayed by a young man that she thought loved her and now her heart is broken.

These are just snapshots of what are usually hours upon hours of counseling. The stories over sixteen years are too numerous to recount and too complicated to go into. The one commonality is the pain. It's in the heart, in the eyes, in the tears, and in the shaky voice. This stuff hurts—really bad.

Have you been hurt? If not, you're in the minority. Along with a culture adrift from biblical principles come big wounds. Because we're so foolish and simple, we make bad decisions that hurt people around us. We inflict pain recklessly and heedlessly.

*Reader's Digest*, June 2006, featured a story about the long-term impact of divorce. Young adults who grew up in divorced homes carried the pain long into their adult lives. The article stated that these "children of divorce" are required to "forge their own values in the intense heat of their own inner lives. They cut a path through the contradictions created by their parents' ways of living." It went on to say that these young people were required to face most of life's problems and forge their own moral beliefs *alone*. The conclusion of the article stated that this generation carries "a heavy burden that shapes their moral identities for years. They also know what they want: a home, a strong marriage… above all they want a secure world for their own children."

Hurt is real. It is undeserved, it is appalling, and it is unthinkable. But it doesn't have to wreck your life. Your past may be littered and scarred with some type of abuse or pain. Your future does not have to be.

Hebrews 12:11–16 speaks loudly to your situation. It begins by using a word we usually associate only with discipline—*chastening*. But the Bible definition of the word is broader. It does include discipline (or chastisement), but it also means training, educating, instruction, and nurture. In other words, your pain has a purpose—all the time, every time! While it may not be disciplinary in nature, it is always *Fatherly*. It is God developing, nurturing, and preparing you for a higher calling and bigger blessings! Isn't that GREAT news?! Read these verses, then we'll talk about them:

> Now no chastening for the present seemeth to be joyous, but grievous: nevertheless afterward it yieldeth the peaceable fruit of righteousness unto them which are exercised thereby. Wherefore lift up the hands which hang down, and the feeble knees; And make straight paths for your feet, lest that which is lame be turned out of the way; but let it rather be healed. Follow peace with all men, and holiness, without which no man shall see the Lord: Looking diligently lest any man fail of the grace of God; lest any root of bitterness springing up trouble you, and thereby many be defiled; Lest there be any fornicator, or profane person, as Esau, who for one morsel of meat sold his birthright.

In this passage, God's desire is to *heal* you and to yield the "peaceable fruit of righteousness" in your life. He says to lift up your hands and your feeble knees. There's hope on the horizon! The past might have hurt really, really bad, but your future can be different. God is in the healing, fruit-bearing business. Would you like to have that peaceable fruit? Would you truly like for your wound to be healed?

***Step one—follow peace with all men.*** Whoever hurt you—forgive them. Whoever is at odds with you—try to make it right. They may not deserve it, and they may not accept it. That's not the issue. *You* are the issue. You want to "see the Lord"—you want to experience His blessings and healing touch in your heart. So, do whatever is in your power to make peace with your past. Forgiveness isn't a feeling or an emotion. It's a daily choice. Over time, your choice to continually forgive will have a tremendous healing effect upon your hurt. Ephesians 4:31–32 says it this way, "Let all bitterness, and wrath, and anger, and clamour, and evil speaking, be put away from you, with all malice: And be ye kind one to another, tenderhearted, forgiving one another, even as God for Christ's sake hath forgiven you."

***Step two—diligently choose God's grace.*** Picture a fork in the road at the point of your pain. One path is called *grace*. One path is called *bitterness*. You must choose which path to walk on. The bitterness path is like an eight-lane road. It's wide and well-traveled. Without any thought, you will end up on this road. The grace path is like a tiny trail that gently and quietly leads the opposite direction. Getting on this path and *staying* on this path requires diligence. In other words, you won't accidentally default to this path. You must choose it again and again. Every day you must wake up and choose the *grace* path.

Grace is God's healing agent in your heart. It's His supernatural ability to heal every hurt and pain and to use it to make you into His unique servant for His unique purpose. Grace is His amazing salve for every wound in your life. Grace changes your disposition—your true character and heart quality—by the power of the Holy Spirit.

If you choose the *bitterness* path, you can read where that leads—to trouble, defilement, fornication, and profanity. Bitterness is folly of enormous destructive proportions. You can't afford to spend any time on this path.

If you look diligently and choose the *grace* path, day by day, God will heal you and use even your painful past to somehow wonderfully bless you in the future. Don't waste another day on the folly of bitterness. If you've been hurt, let God begin healing you right now. Choose grace.

***Step three—keep choosing God's grace for the rest of your life.*** Let me give you a quick formula for exactly what I'm talking about when I say "choose God's grace."

Recently, I gave a hurting young man a "spiritual prescription." I told him that I couldn't take away his hurt, but that God could, and that God would use it to bless him in the future if he would choose grace. In an effort to spell out clearly what "choosing grace" means, I gave him this list of biblical truths. I urged him to carry it in his wallet and to read and pray over it every morning.

Here's the list:

---

1. *I'm saved—I'm on my way to Heaven through Christ!*
2. *I'm highly valuable, wanted, and important to God!*
3. *God has a great plan for my future!*
4. *God will give me strength for today if I ask for it!*
5. *I will honor God and my parents today!*
6. *God, please be my best friend today!*
7. *God, please give me **grace** today!*

---

I share it with you not because the list is anything special, but because choosing grace is a daily decision to accept God's truth about what you're going through. God's grace is real, and when you ask for it diligently (over and over again, day after day), He heals you with it!

I'm certainly not minimizing your hurt, but do you want to spend the rest of your life licking your wounds? Wouldn't you like to shake off the wounds of others and move on to maturity by God's grace? You can.

Choose grace. Choose healing. Bitterness is folly.

In the midst of a generation of fools in their folly, be wise. In a generation consumed with simplicity, be understanding. Embrace the Bible, the God of the Bible, and His paths of righteousness. If you must run—run to wisdom. If you must flee—flee to God. If you must find your individuality—realize you can only find it with God. Break the mold of your generation. Swim upstream. Take the path of most resistance.

Folly is different for all of us, but remember that distraction, fear, selfish desires, and bitterness are always folly—for all of us.

I have a feeling that you're smarter than a Siberian husky. Don't run to folly. Run to wisdom! Your culture won't know what to do with you, but you'll know what to do with your life! And that's what matters.

On a side note, I promise that the rattlesnake story was our last snake illustration. This book is starting to creep me out!

*Then I saw that wisdom
excelleth folly, as far as light
excelleth darkness.*
—ECCLESIASTES 2:13

# CHAPTER FOUR

# DEATH BY CIDER

*Getting Back Up on the Two Feet of Truth*

A few years ago, my wife took the kids to visit Grandpa and Grandma just after Christmas. This particular year, I wasn't able to go, which left me home alone. I really hate being home alone—no noise, no wife, no food being prepared, no one to talk to. It's something like solitary confinement for my soul.

On this particular "home alone" experience, I decided to try to pull together some lunch from our Christmas leftovers. The first thing that caught my eye in the refrigerator was a half-empty bottle of sparkling cider—one of our holiday family favorites. I picked up the bottle, shook it a little to make sure that it was still carbonated, and set it on the counter. Then I filled a plate with turkey, mashed potatoes, and stuffing, and tossed it into the microwave. A few moments later, my dinner was hot and ready, and I was preparing to sit down, watch some news, and try to occupy my mind in an empty house.

Then, out of nowhere—BOOM—a gunshot rang out in my kitchen. I mean this was loud! It was so loud and so close, I instinctively and immediately dropped flat to the floor. I expected to hear glass shatter. I waited for the intruder to shout his demands.

One shot—that's all there was, followed by an eerie silence. Everything was deathly still—except my heart, which happened to be pounding loud enough for the neighbors three doors down to hear it.

Several moments passed. My food was getting cold. Finally, I climbed to my knees and crawled over to the kitchen window. I peered fearfully through the blinds— nothing. I crawled on hands and knees into the dining and living room, stopping to peer out each window while trying not to give away my carefully hidden position— still nothing. After crawling full-circle through the entire downstairs of my home, I managed to gain the courage to stand up—the whole while moving slowly, ready to hit the deck again at the slightest sound. This time I walked through the house, slowly and methodically inspecting all potential hiding places.

By now I'm starting to question my sanity. I *know* I didn't *imagine* this! After a few more moments I decided to take a huge risk and venture outside. Slowly, I cracked the door, peered out, and stepped into the afternoon sun. The street was quiet. Not a car, not a pedestrian, not a neighbor— nothing was out of place. I circled the house. Nothing. I was as puzzled as I have ever been.

A few moments later, I'm back at the kitchen counter, catching my breath, reheating my food, pouring my sparkling cider, and wondering if I could have possibly imagined this. That's when I noticed. The top was gone. The sparkling cider had no white pop-top like it had a moment before. A few feet away, in the middle of the family room, there it lay, and that's when the little light bulb came on in my head. (I'm not sure what would have hurt worse—death by gunshot or finding out just how stupid I really was.)

My "gunshot" was nothing more than the pressure that had built up in that bottle after I had shaken it. My intruder—non-existent. My fear—unfounded.

In much the same way, many young adults of this culture find themselves scared frozen, deceived by selfish desires, distracted by folly, and distressed by past pain. They refuse to stand and face the future because of some errant imagination. They are dealing with the lies of their own emotions. They've been crippled and disabled by a culture that tells them to stay youthfully irresponsible. Fear tells them to avoid adulthood and real maturity.

If you identify with these emotions, *you too* are being deceived. One day, if you snap out of it, you're going to laugh at the folly that almost robbed you of your future.

I've had no less than one hundred young adults in recent years tell me, "I'm afraid to grow up." Sometimes their parents see it first. They often sit across from my desk or in my car or at a restaurant, stare blankly or tearfully, and admit that when they face the future it scares them to death. Can you identify?

> *Embrace the future with passion, anticipation, excitement, and hope!*

You must stare down that fear and realize it is fake. It is founded in a lie. You must look through it, beyond it, and see God's reality.

The Apostle Paul wrote of his prayer for the Christians at Ephesus, "Cease not to give thanks for you, making mention of you in my prayers; That the God of our Lord Jesus Christ, the Father of glory, may give unto you the spirit of wisdom and revelation in the knowledge of him: The eyes of your understanding being enlightened; that ye may know what is the hope of his calling, and what the riches of the glory of his inheritance in the saints" (Ephesians 1:16–18).

Paul was praying that God would give them wisdom and revelation to see what they couldn't see. He wanted the "eyes of their understanding" to be enlightened, primarily so that they could see "the hope of his calling" and "the riches of the glory of his inheritance in the saints." Paul was saying, "You're blinded to God's rewards!" He knew their whole perspective would change if they could see the truth.

Young adults of this generation are afraid to grow up for one simple reason. They are believing lies. When your eyes open and God allows you to see the "hope of his calling"— you will run forward in life! You will seize this day and the next! You will embrace the future with passion, anticipation, excitement, and hope!

For me, the difference between a peaceful, post-Christmas lunch and a panicked, paranoid freak show was simply one word—TRUTH. I believed a lie, and my heart, hair, and knees paid the price. Heart—because it nearly stopped beating, hair—because some of it fell out that day, and knees—because they hurt after all that crawling!

This is why Jesus said, "And ye shall know the truth, and the truth shall make you free" (John 8:32). Truth changes things! Knowing the truth matters. It gives you a reality check. Just as knowing the truth about my "gunshot" brought me back to reality, even so, knowing the truth about your future and God's will can bring you back to hope, courage, and forward motion!

God says, "The law of the LORD is perfect, converting the soul: the testimony of the LORD is sure, making wise the simple" (Psalm 19:7). Again He says, "The entrance of thy words giveth light; it giveth understanding unto the simple" (Psalm 119:130). "For the commandment is a lamp; and the law is light" (Proverbs 6:23).

In other words, God's truth gives understanding. God's Word will shine the light on the lies of culture. God's laws will guide you and establish your heart in reality.

## Making the Most of Your Vapor

Life is short. You probably don't believe that yet, but it is. God created your life to appear and disappear rather quickly, and He has given you some pretty important things to accomplish while you're here. "Whereas ye know not what shall be on the morrow. For what is your life? It is even a vapour, that appeareth for a little time, and then vanisheth away" (James 4:14).

The Apostle Paul wrote this charge to the Christians at Ephesus, "Wherefore he saith, Awake thou that sleepest, and arise from the dead, and Christ shall give thee light. See then that ye walk circumspectly, not as fools, but as wise, Redeeming the time, because the days are evil. Wherefore be ye not unwise, but understanding what the will of the Lord is. And be not drunk with wine, wherein is excess; but be filled with the Spirit" (Ephesians 5:14-18).

In other words, wake up! Come out of your cultural coma. Step into the light that Christ offers you and walk circumspectly in life. *Circumspectly* simply means to live carefully observant in every direction. Be aware of where you're headed, what's around you, and where the traps are. Be wise! Fools don't walk circumspectly; they walk with their heads down, ready to be blindsided at any moment. God wants you to live a life that is aware, awake, and alert.

Then he says, "Redeeming the time, because the days are evil...understanding what the will of the Lord is." This philosophy is the exact opposite of your culture's. Culture tells you that you have "all the time in the world—stay stupid a while longer"; but God says time is running out— redeem or recapture the time and live right! Understand what the will of the Lord is and live it now while you have the chance.

Do you get it? You don't have a spare decade. You don't even have a spare month or a spare week! Every moment matters! Every day matters! God's plan for you is now. Don't waste another day on foolishness and folly.

And so, it's time to turn a corner—both in this book and in your life. We've spent enough time inspecting the problem. We've seen the mentality of a culture adrift. We've studied the stupidity of the simple, the folly of the foolish, and the scourge of the scornful. It's time to see the truth.

You don't have to spend your young adult life crawling around, emotionally crippled and wishing you could stay immature and irresponsible. While your culture is distracted by lies and imagined fears, you can stand back up on two feet, plant yourself in the will of God, and step forward with courage. In fact—*you must*!

In the coming chapters, you must see what you will miss if you keep crawling around on the floor of life, peering through the windows of childhood, hiding from the imagined fears of the future. You must immediately begin to courageously embrace God's plan for your adult life. Determine to see the reality about adult life—it's worth it.

Let's move on.

And by the way, watch out for those little white pop-tops on the sparkling cider bottles! Those things sound like they can kill!

# PART TWO

# WHAT'S WAITING FOR YOU?

*The Rewards of
Embracing Adulthood*

# WHAT'S WAITING FOR YOU?

*Peter Pan didn't want to grow up, but he didn't realize what he was missing. Adult pressures, adult responsibilities, adult life is flat worth it if you do it right! Braving adulthood is extremely rewarding and abundantly joyful.*

*Ignoring the future doesn't work—it still shows up. It's like a freight train barreling down the tracks toward you—you can jump on and enjoy the ride, or you can get run over. There's no ignoring it.*

*If the richest man in America called you right now and said, "There are some big rewards just ahead in your life if you do what I say..." would you listen? Well, think bigger. God is calling, and He offers bigger rewards for living life the right way! Will you listen?*

## CHAPTER FIVE

# A MAN CAN'T JUST SIT AROUND

*Reward #1—A Life of Eternal Significance*

"I don't care about anything."

The words fell like death from the lips of a young man in the prime of his youth. Somewhere in his teen years his heart had been drained of life by godless influences of music, media, and friends. He had no reason to get out of bed. No reason to care. No reason to really embrace life—or so he thought.

Rarely have I seen such total apathy and lifelessness in a young adult. A few moments later, as an afterthought, he said, "Life is a lot easier when you don't care about anything."

I did my best during our appointment to refute his errant thought processes. Sure, life is easier if you don't care about anything, but that's like saying life is easier if you don't *feel* anything.

The last time I couldn't "feel anything" was after a long morning at the dentist. I had four fillings on one side of my mouth and it was completely numb! But I was hungry too! For some reason a slurpee or a fruit smoothie just didn't cut it. I needed real food, numb face or not. So I went against the wise admonitions of my dentist, my wife, and my better judgment. I ordered a steak sandwich with all the trimmings! Was it good? You bet! It was awesome! I can't remember the last time a sandwich tasted so good.

Until that fateful moment when I picked up my napkin and wiped my lips—that's when I saw the blood. You guessed it! Idiot-man here was chewing his lip in the middle of all that delicious steak and onion mix. Quickly surveying the damage, I discovered my well-chewed bottom lip and returned to "fruit-smoothie-ville." My wife didn't feel sorry for me either—she had tried to warn me.

So there I was—fruit smoothie in one hand, bloody napkin in the other, chewed-up lip dangling loosely, and a delicious steak sandwich going to waste before my very eyes. This was not good. Yet, the good news is, I didn't feel a thing! I was numb.

A few hours later the medication wore off, and feeling returned with a vengeance! Pain gripped my lower lip like never before, and it stayed there for a solid week. A few hours of numbness and a few premature bites of a steak and lip sandwich cost me days of pain and regret.

Even so, Satan is aggressively numbing the hearts of young adults and leading them into a general apathy about life. While they are numb, the damage is done and the pain is not far off. If you are convinced that the future isn't worth caring about, I challenge you to wake up. In your numbness, you're going to bite yourself and live the rest of your life regretting it.

God puts it this way, "And that, knowing the time, that now it is high time to awake out of sleep" (Romans 13:11). "Awake to righteousness, and sin not; for some have not the knowledge of God: I speak this to your shame" (1 Corinthians 15:34). "Wherefore he saith, Awake thou that sleepest, and arise from the dead, and Christ shall give thee light" (Ephesians 5:14).

Life is worth caring about! Life *matters*. How you live, what you do, and who you become matters for all of eternity. The pain of "not caring" will eventually catch up with you after the Novocaine of youthfulness has worn off! In that moment, you *will* care! You will care with all of your heart, but then it will be too late. You don't get to rewind life and live it again. You only get one chance to live right. The choices you make today matter forever.

## The Things We Do for Significance

Have you ever noticed the stupid things people do to get attention? In 2006, wealthy businessman Mark Ecko spent a small fortune to be noticed. He secretly rented a 747 jet airliner, parked it in a hangar in Riverside, California, and hired a team of people to paint one side of it to match Air Force One perfectly. All those involved in the prank were sworn to secrecy. Once the paint job was complete, he hired a film crew and video taped a group of hooded actors climbing fences, sneaking past guards, and tagging the President's plane with spray paint. In the end, the video was posted on the Internet and fooled even the United States military. The airlift wing that operates Air Force One literally checked the real plane just to be sure. It was all a hoax—a very expensive one, but apparently worth the feelings of notoriety for Mr. Ecko.

In 1982, Larry Walters made history as the first and only man to ever enter restricted airspace at LAX airport on a lawn chair tied to weather balloons!

Sitting in his North Hollywood backyard one day, with nothing to do, Larry decided to tie helium-filled weather balloons to his lawn chair to see if he could make it fly. In all, he used forty-five four-foot weather balloons, and sure enough, he had "lift-off." For his journey, he packed some soft drinks, sandwiches, a camera, a CB radio, and a pellet gun, so he could pop the balloons and descend back to earth.

Moments later, things went wrong as Larry ascended much higher than anticipated—16,000 feet to be exact! Now afraid to shoot the balloons, Larry drifted into the primary approach corridor of the Los Angeles International Airport where an incoming pilot radioed the tower that he had just passed a man in a lawn chair at 16,000 feet.

Fourteen hours later, Larry finally shot a couple of balloons and began a slow descent into a Long Beach neighborhood. He was immediately arrested, fined, and given a national spotlight on news programs and late-night TV shows. When asked why he attempted this crazy stunt, he simply replied, "A man can't just sit around!"

From preschool antics to Hollywood show business to the latest high-speed chase on the evening news—people will go to great and sometimes ridiculous lengths to be noticed and to fill their heart's yearning for significance. We crave *importance*. We long to know that our lives matter to someone, somewhere. As long as we feel valued and important, we feel worthwhile.

We want to be loved and valued. It's in us. We can't escape it because God put it there. Most people live their whole lives searching for this significance and never truly find it. Yet, *you* have the privilege of discovering significance *now*—early in life—and living the rest of your life basking in it!

The first great reward of courageously moving forward into your adult life is *eternal significance*. Those two words are really big in scope, and I must admit I've struggled for weeks with how to adequately communicate them to you. This truth penetrates to the deepest needs and cravings of our hearts and reaches into the unfathomable vastness of eternity. This truth is bigger than our ability to comprehend it—and trying to wrestle with it is something like my two dogs trying to discuss Einstein's theory of relativity. So,

I'm going to bark for a while, and you try to understand. Better yet, ask the Lord right now to enlarge your heart and enlighten your understanding as we look into His Word.

## REWARD #1
## ETERNAL SIGNIFICANCE

A search for significance is what makes you get out of bed in the morning. It is the "why" behind everything you do. Why do you want friends? Why do you work? Why do you get an education? Somewhere at the core of all of these questions is a deep, heart-level quest for a life that matters. Your heart craves significance like your lungs crave oxygen and your stomach craves lunch. You want to be important to somebody. We all do. And more than we realize, this heart desire drives our lives and our decisions.

The scary part of this desire for significance is that the world cannot fulfill it. Oh, it tries! The devil is great at making lofty promises and dangling carrots of significance in our young faces, but all worldly pursuits of significance end in emptiness and spiritual starvation. The world will take your desire for significance, put an emotional ring through your nose and lead you around like a dog. You will spend your life chasing shadows of fulfillment but never really finding it—like that pot of gold that doesn't exist at the end of every rainbow.

Yet, when you courageously embrace God and His purpose, you find it. Like a surprise birthday party, it kind of catches you off guard. You might call it a fringe benefit of loving and living for God. He is the only One who can fill the longing for significance in your heart. You have a God-shaped hole in your heart that only He can fill.

## You Matter to God

What is your picture of God? Some people view Him as a heavenly judge waiting to pour out punishment and condemnation. Some picture Him as a grandfather on a rocking chair, drifting off to sleep while the universe goes on without His intervention. Some view Him as some non-descript, intangible force of both good and evil—in everything and everyone. Yet none of these is how He describes Himself.

In His Word, He describes Himself to His children as a loving Heavenly Father—a God of love, provision, protection, and refuge. He calls Himself our strong tower, our shelter, and our rock. He describes Himself as pursuing our hearts, desiring our love, loving us enough to die for us, and abounding in mercy and grace towards us. He tells us that He is waiting to forgive us, redeem us, renew us, and adopt us as His own. He promises us His protection, His provision, His power, and His perfect will.

On every page of His Word, God's heart longs for us to love Him, follow Him, and honor Him. Throughout Scripture, His cry is for us to *trust* Him—to *faith* Him. He desires for us to be His people. He delights when we call Him our God. This book could not contain enough pages to adequately describe the heart of God for you. He is "crazy about you" and there's never a moment of any day that He isn't thinking about you. You have one hundred percent of His undivided attention all the time. He knows everything there is to know about you—your past, your present, your future, even your private thoughts—and yet He can't take His eyes off you. You have riveted His attention, and He won't ever stop pursuing a personal relationship with you.

It would be impressive to discover that the governor of your state knew your name and valued you as a friend. It would be over the top to think that the President of the United States considered you a close companion—a personal friend. How much more significant is it to find out that you matter to GOD?!

Have you ever wondered what He is thinking about you? He tells us very clearly. One of my favorite passages that describes God's heart is found in Jeremiah 24. After showing Jeremiah two baskets of figs, one decayed and rotten and the other pure and ripe, God compares His faithful children to the good figs. Here's what He says:

> Thus saith the LORD, the God of Israel; Like these good figs, so will I acknowledge them that are carried away captive of Judah, whom I have sent out of this place into the land of the Chaldeans for their good. For I will set mine eyes upon them for good, and I will bring them again to this land: and I will build them, and not pull them down; and I will plant them, and not pluck them up. And I will give them an heart to know me, that I am the LORD: and they shall be my people, and I will be their God: for they shall return unto me with their whole heart.—JEREMIAH 24:5-7

A few chapters later, He speaks of His good plans again:

> For thus saith the LORD, That after seventy years be accomplished at Babylon I will visit you, and perform my good word toward you, in causing you to return to this place. For I know the thoughts that I think toward you, saith the LORD, thoughts of peace, and not of evil, to give you an expected end. Then shall ye call upon me, and ye shall go and pray unto me, and I will hearken unto you. And ye shall seek me, and find me, when ye shall search for me with all your heart.
> —JEREMIAH 29:10-13

Do you see God's amazing heart for His children in these passages? Do you see His character towards those who choose Him? Just reading these words would be enough for me to "sign up for life"! This is the God that my heart craves! This is the Almighty Creator who made my heart!

He's not only thinking of me, He's thinking good thoughts. He's been in a heavenly planning session laying out His good plans for my life.

He says in these passages that He *acknowledges* us, which literally means He recognizes us, looks intently at us with respect or reverence! That's how God is looking at you. Then He says, "I will set mine eyes upon them for good...." Do you get it? Remember the look that your parents would give you just before you opened your Christmas gifts or just before you blew out your birthday candles? That's the look! He has it for you, right now! Then He says, "I will bring them...I will build them...I will plant them...I will give them...." What a God! He's planning to guide you, build you, establish you, and cultivate your life to bear fruit to His glory. Just knowing that God has gone to this much effort and planning on my behalf moves me to humble surrender.

Then God does the impossible—the unthinkable—the unimaginable! He says, "I will replace your heart with a heart that desires to know me, and then we will pursue each other, know each other, and belong to each other." God isn't commanding you to "make your heart to know me." He's offering to do that work for you. He's offering to swap out your heart with one that loves Him deeply. Then He paints a picture that looks something like this:

"I will be your God—your everything. I will protect, provide, guide, love, nurture, and care for you. I will give you all of myself forever. And you will be mine. I will have your whole heart, your whole love. I long for you and you long for me. Let us love each other and fully give our hearts to each other. Together, we will be fully each other's for all of eternity. I will be your God, and you will be my people."

Sounds like the perfect marriage, doesn't it? It is. It's the only perfect marriage that will ever exist. God invites you to be the bride, and He's the groom! Could your heart ever find a greater love or a greater significance? Could you find a greater promise or a more delightful future anywhere else?

But He doesn't stop there. It gets better. In chapter 29, He continues unabashedly unveiling His passionate heart for you. He says that He's thinking thoughts of peace to bring you to an expected end—a quest with a delightful destination! Those words *expected end* literally mean an arrival at the things you've hoped for or the fulfillment of the deepest longings of your heart. Are you falling in love with this God as much as I am?

> *People who run from God just don't know Him.*

He goes on to promise you that His ear is bent towards you. He says, "When you call, I'm right here listening and answering. When you seek me, I'm right here waiting! I am your God, you are my child—let's go through all of life and eternity this way." What an amazing invitation!

Do you get it? This is not a God that one would run from, and those who do just don't know Him. It's like little kids at Disneyland who cry and scream because Mickey Mouse scares them! They just don't know him. Mickey's a pretty nice guy, once you get past the initial shock of the size of his ears. It took each of my kids a couple of trips, but now they generally run to him, hug him, and gladly take their photos with him. (Well, my twelve and fifteen-year-olds have moved beyond that phase, but Haylee is still there.)

When you read of a God of judgment, anger, and vengeance in the Bible, you are reading of a passionate love that God has for your heart! His anger is toward sin and toward those who willfully choose sin and deny Him. It is righteous, just, and fair. If He didn't love you so passionately, He wouldn't need to hate sin so vehemently. In other words, His fiery love for you mandates His fiery anger towards your enemy. His heart toward you, His child, is one of immeasurable love and gentleness.

Should you fear Him the way that a murderer fears the electric chair? No. You should fear Him the way a precious child rightly fears a loving father. It's a completely different kind of fear—one based upon love, honor, reverence, and closeness.

Once you get past the size of God's power and the fierceness of His righteous anger, you discover that He truly is awesome! You fall deeply in love with Him, and you want nothing more than to be His child, in His care, living out His plan, enjoying His provision for the rest of your life. Why would anyone run from this wonderful Heavenly Father? They just don't know Him.

*God made you on purpose, for a purpose.*

Quite honestly, I could write forever about this unimaginable God. He's truly indescribable. You're just going to have to find out for yourself, because I have a page limit here. So, let me get back on point.

There are three simple thoughts that you should soak up from these verses in Jeremiah. Let your heart bask in these truths, perhaps for the first time. Relish them. Fall in love with a God who is madly in love with you!

***First of all, God thinks of you!*** Stop and think about it, and be amazed. You are on His mind. You should be awed as the psalmist was, "What is man, that thou art mindful of him?" (Psalm 8:4).

When was the last time you thought of even *one* of the ants living in your backyard? When was the last time you expressed concern for one of them, fought to rescue one, or promised to provide for one? When was the last time you sacrificed so an ant could have a better life? Have you written them, reached out to them, cried out to them? If you have—well, we won't go there. I think you get my point. This is *God*, and He's thinking of *you*! He actually loves you, longs for you, and desires you. But wait, it gets better.

***Second, God thinks good of you!*** He's not just thinking about you, He's thinking good thoughts. He's not mad at you, angry with you, or waiting to catch you doing something wrong. He already punished His Son for all of your sins, and they were washed clean and removed as far as the east is from the west the moment you trusted Him! Now, He sets His eyes and His thoughts upon you for *good*. He envisions an incredible future for you—an expected end. In other words, raise your expectations if you go with God in life! Expect a better life and a better end! Expect the ultimate desires of your heart to be fulfilled in a most extravagant way.

When was the last time you actually planned a fun day for the ants in your backyard—like a birthday party, a field trip, or a weekend get-away? Ridiculous? Not as ridiculous as God making good plans for my life and yours. We're dirt. We're nothing special. We mess up our lives; we reject God's commands; we hurt each other; and we don't even last long. Left to ourselves, we get dirty, smelly, and sickly. We break easily, tire quickly, and foul up regularly. We are self-centered, demanding, and petty—and we're constantly just one breath or one misstep away from death. Frankly, we're a mess. We have absolutely nothing to offer, but we matter to God. In His sight, we are fearfully and wonderfully made in His image. He spanned all of time and eternity to die for us and rescue us.

You matter to God. You are on His mind, and He's smiling. You are in His plans, and He's anticipating. You are in His eyes, and He's winking. You were His first, last, and every thought today. You are His workmanship created in Christ Jesus. You are His creation, His child, His treasure, and His delight. He made you on purpose for a purpose. He's molding you every moment of every day. He's making you into a masterpiece in His grand design for time and eternity. He's infatuated with you!

Are you feeling significant yet? Do you realize how important you must be if you matter this much to God? Kind of puts a different light on life, doesn't it?

***Third, God has developed an awesome plan for your life!*** God doesn't just call you a servant but a friend. He doesn't just plan your life, but He desires to bring you in on a much bigger plan. Picture it this way: you're not just a kid with toys who lives at the White House where lots of important stuff happens in your dad's world. You are a co-laborer who is a part of major world events! You are invited into the bigger picture of time and eternity, and you play a significant role in God's master plan. How cool is that?

When was the last time you included your backyard ants on anything that mattered? When's the last time that your plans hinged on them? Since when did their feelings matter, their thoughts have value, or their role have significance in your life? I doubt you mentioned them in your high school graduation speech. I doubt you would honor their memory in your autobiography. Ants are most likely insignificant to your life or future.

So, why would God include us in His plan? Why would He open His heart to humanity at all, much less you and me? Yet, that's what He does. He invites you into His master plan to play a critical role, to carry responsibilities that He created you to fulfill. Why would you settle for some silly, sidelining career in your own miniscule plan? What could possibly be attractive about the monotonous cycle of sleeping, working, paying bills, eating, and doing it all over again day after day for no important reason? You are invited into the cabinet room of the universe to partner with your Heavenly Father in an eternal mission that matters! This is HUGE!

By now, I want to courageously embrace my own young adult life, and I'm not a young adult anymore!

But there's one more thought you must grasp in this chapter.

## You Matter to Others

Yes, you matter to God and to His plan. But you matter to others too—and I'm not talking about your parents and friends—though I'm sure you matter to them.

You matter to people you haven't met yet—people in your future—people you may never meet if you don't go forward in faith. I'm talking about your spouse, your kids, your grandkids, and perhaps the thousands of people with whom God will intersect your life in the future. These are people that God has pre-determined to place under your influence. The outcome of their lives will hinge upon your impact. The course of history will be written by how you influence them.

Recently, I was delivering a message about the power of generational influence. To illustrate my point I asked my twelve-year-old son, Larry, to stand next to me representing the next generation. Then I asked a man in his forties to stand next to Larry. Picture a line up of three people—me, my son, and a full-grown man on the other side of Larry.

At this point I told the congregation that Larry is my son (the next generation), and the man on the other side represents Larry's son (the generation to follow). The room broke into immediate laughter. It was somewhat of a ridiculous picture, but powerful nonetheless. People laugh at that illustration simply because they don't picture twelve-year-old kids having forty-year-old children. Yet, every forty-year-old was once twelve, and every forty-year-old's father was once twelve. If Jesus tarries in His coming, most likely, you will one day have a forty-year-old child and eventually a forty-year-old grandchild!

Let this sink in for a moment. The lives of those who come after you will be built upon the foundation of *your* decisions. How you live, who you are, and the choices you make *now* impact them *then*. They need you to courageously embrace God's plan. They need you to be everything that

God wants you to be. They are depending upon you to do the right thing *now*.

The people of Israel wandered in the wilderness for forty years because of ten faithless, heartless spies. An entire generation of people died in the desert because of the previous generation's decisions. Lot's family sank into generational decline and destruction because he "pitched his tent toward Sodom," refusing to resolve conflict with his Uncle Abraham. I doubt he intended to ruin his kids' lives when his herdsmen were griping against Abraham's herdsmen. He was too young and immature to think that far ahead. I doubt those spies had a clue that they were condemning their children to forty wasted years and themselves to a God-forsaken death. They didn't see the bigger picture. They didn't understand that their decisions mattered to others.

What fate are you sealing for those coming behind you? What bad decisions are you making now that will reap a harvest in your children and grandchildren? Your life is far bigger than just you. Get over yourself—and quickly. Get your eyes on the horizon and live with a heart for those you will one day love.

If you live for folly and sink deeper into the cesspool of self-centeredness, you're going to hurt those coming behind you. Your choices matter to them. Your decisions matter for generations to come. For their sake, step up to adulthood, courageously embrace wisdom and responsibility, and live right—on purpose for God's purpose. Choose to grow. Choose to go forward. You matter to others.

## Life Will Drop You Hard, But God Won't

John Sutter was a man of many interests, abilities, and connections. He was one of the first Americans to settle in the territory of California when it was still controlled by

Mexico in the early 1800s. He established Sutter's Fort in central California, which eventually became Sacramento.

John was quite the entrepreneur. He obtained land from Mexico, entered into friendly labor agreements with hostile Indians, and made major advancements in the early development of the Sacramento area. In the 1840s, John decided to invest into constructing a lumber mill up river from his fort where he could produce lumber and float it down river to accommodate the rapid expansion of central California all the way to San Francisco.

He didn't want gold—he wanted lumber. He wasn't chasing metal—he was developing land and establishing a civilization. He was a man of grand plans and aggressive vision. Through it all, he never anticipated, in his wildest imaginations, the strange and tragic turn that his life would suddenly take in one fateful morning.

It was January 24, 1848, and John's sawmill on the American River was becoming a reality in the hills of central California. He had hired a man named John Marshall to handle the construction project. Early that morning, Marshall was checking the mill's tailrace to make sure it was clear of debris when something caught his eye. Perhaps it was the way the sunlight reflected off the objects in the water, but something caused John to take a closer look.

Resting at the water bottom were the first nuggets of gold discovered in California. Good news for John Sutter, one might think. Suspecting that these rocks were gold, Marshall bagged the find, said nothing to his workers, and immediately took his discovery to John Sutter—his boss and the owner of the land and the mill.

After a few secret consultations, Sutter confirmed that these nuggets were indeed gold of the highest quality—and what unfolded next, no one could have predicted. He attempted to keep his discovery quiet just long enough to finish construction on the sawmill—the key to his future financial stability. He envisioned his workers leaving and his mill never being completed because of a rush for gold. He wasn't willing to risk his financial future on a few stray nuggets.

Sadly, in just a few days, the secret leaked, news reached San Francisco, and life forever changed for John Sutter. The historic California Gold Rush had begun. Almost immediately, hoards of violent and greedy people descended upon John's quiet fort and land claims up river. His land, his mill, and his claim to any gold was completely overrun and pillaged by claim jumpers, squatters, and vagrants in search of quick fortune.

A lot of gold was discovered in California in the coming years, and a lot of people struck it rich. A lot of money was made, but John Sutter never saw any of it. He was ruined in a matter of months and never recovered. The man instrumental in the early founding of Sacramento, the settling of central California, and the historic discovery of gold was dropped like a hot potato by history itself and died bankrupt, disappointed, and in poverty nearly forty years later.

Near the end of his life, Sutter appealed to the US government for compensation for his role in the events that literally shaped California and in some sense, the entire country. He died a few days before Congress turned him down. Death, then denial—could it get any worse? In his appeal to Congress, he wrote these words:

"By this sudden discovery of the gold, all my great plans were destroyed. Had I succeeded for a few years before the gold was discovered, I would have been the richest citizen on the Pacific shore; but it had to be different. Instead of being rich, I am ruined...."

Life without God is completely unpredictable and insecure. You will spend your life chasing significance only to end up empty-handed. Like John Sutter, you could have the good fortune of the world at your fingertips. You could have the best-laid plans and grandest dreams. But without

God, it will all come to naught, and your heart will be severely disappointed.

Solomon gave himself to know folly, and at the end, it left him destitute. Significance is only found in God. Eternal purpose is only found in His will. Everything else is a rabbit trail leading to nowhere. You could discover gold without God, but even then, Satan's claim jumpers will leave you spiritually bankrupt.

The psalmist wrote, "Thou wilt shew me the path of life: in thy presence is fulness of joy; at thy right hand there are pleasures for evermore" (Psalm 16:11). Only in God's presence will you find your heart's deepest desire. When God called Abraham to Himself, He said it this way, "Fear not, Abram: I am thy shield, and thy exceeding great reward" (Genesis 15:1). What a great God! The more you know Him, the more you will love Him.

The first incredible reward of courageously embracing God's plan for your life is *eternal significance*. You can be an overgrown couch potato for the next ten years, or you can live up to your value in God's eyes. You can partner with your Creator in His eternal plan and accept the fact that you are significant to Him.

> *The more you know Him, the more you will love Him.*

You matter to God. You matter to God's plan. You matter to others. What greater reward could you have—the deepest longing of your heart fulfilled by your loving Heavenly Father?

As misguided as he may have been, Larry Walters had it right in one way: "A man can't just sit around." You weren't created to vegetate. Your design doesn't allow you to find fulfillment in apathy. You crave purpose and significance. Thankfully, you don't need to soar to 16,000 feet in a lawn chair to be noticed. You don't need to discover gold to find happiness. You need to discover God. He has already noticed you, and He's so taken by you that He can't take His eyes off you!

The world will pick you up and drop you hard, just like it did John Sutter. God will never do that to you. He is your refuge. He is the hand that catches you when the world drops you. In Him, you will truly find the full significance that your heart craves!

## CHAPTER SIX

# WHEN BIG THINGS MEAN NOTHING AND EVERYTHING MEANS SOMETHING

*Reward #2—The Timeless Gifts of a Good Life*

Transitioning from youth into adulthood can sometimes be like getting a bucket of cold water thrown on you during a hot shower—jolting, to say the least. Why would anyone desire that kind of "wake-up call" in life? What if I could prove to you that such "jolts" are the foreshocks of major blessings from God? What if God awakens us so that He can bless us in greater ways? I believe He does just that, and it was early in my twenties when I began to experience my first few "buckets of cold water."

Dana and I were just getting our feet on the ground in our marriage and ministry; we had just graduated from Bible college and moved across country; and we were expecting our first child. While we were greatly blessed in many ways, one of the most difficult challenges of our young lives was transportation. Our cars were breaking down a lot and were costing more to fix than we could afford. At the same time, I didn't see how our budget could possibly handle a new car payment or even a used car payment.

One discouraging afternoon, Dana called me in tears from the parking lot of a local grocery store. She was stranded again with a car that wouldn't start. She was eight months along, it was hot outside, and I felt like a total loser. I knew I had to do something, but I was at a loss for what. One bucket of cold water, coming right up!

That evening, I called my dad to get his perspective and advice. I don't remember all the conversation, but I do remember him saying two things that I desperately needed to hear. Just as I started to complain about my circumstances, he interrupted me and flatly said, "Hey, wait a minute! You're the one who wanted to get married and play house! This comes with the territory."

Splash!!

Heartless? No. Exactly what I needed. He confronted me with my own decisions and challenged me to step up to the plate. Then he said, "Cary, it's your responsibility as a husband and a leader to provide your wife with safe and reliable transportation, and God hasn't left you alone in this. He promises that He will provide, but you're going to have to take on the responsibility for your own family and do the right thing."

*The rewards of adult life are far better than the irresponsibility of youth.*

You might think I'm stupid, but I needed to hear that. As a young adult, I needed to be infused with a good dose of courage and faith. I needed the jolt. I needed to be hit in the face with the truth.

Throughout my twenties, I could point to many such jolting experiences—key "growing-up" moments. As you move forward with God, you can expect the same types of experiences—moments of truth when you are called to faith in action—moments when you are required to do the right thing even though it's painful and uncertain. These pressures of adult life can sometimes be overwhelming and can make you wish you were still sixteen. In the heat of such a trial or a growing moment, you are tempted to run for cover, but you must know this—in such moments you are on a crash course with God's greatest gifts if you will proceed forward. The rewards of adult life are far better than the irresponsibility of youth.

Back to my story. There was a time in my teens when my parents handled all my transportation needs. They shuttled me to and from school and events. They took care of gas, insurance, registration, vehicle maintenance, and vehicle purchasing. These things never entered my conscious thought. I just sat down, buckled up, and enjoyed the ride. Sometime after I turned sixteen, we purchased a '65 VW Bug. Even then, my responsibilities were somewhat minimal. I washed and drove the car, but Dad still owned it, paid for the maintenance, and paid the registration. Life was good then.

After college, marriage, and ministry, I felt that I was suddenly "on my own." But I wasn't. And that's the point. I felt alone in this responsibility, but little did I know that God was way ahead of me. He was simply growing me and preparing me for something better than my broken down cars.

Some days after that phone call, and after much prayer, I decided that we would buy a car. Beyond that, I was clueless. I felt like a blind man grasping for a guiding hand—somewhat lost in a sea of options. Yet, God reached out of Heaven and grabbed that grasping hand and guided me to the right decision.

Here's the conclusion of the matter. The Lord allowed us to sell both of our aging cars and led us to a nicer used car with low miles and a low price tag. We qualified for a low car payment, which we somewhat fearfully accepted, and God gave us reliable transportation. The real miracle of provision in this story is, that car never broke down for the five years that we owned it. We drove it until it was paid for and sold it for top dollar to give an offering back to the Lord five years later. We never missed a payment, and every day since then the Lord has provided for our transportation.

I learned a major lesson in that bucket of cold water—God has called me forward into major responsibility, including providing for my family, but He has not called me to go *alone*! He has already determined to fill my life with good gifts if I will trust Him. He promises to provide, if I will go forward courageously. Did I have to step up in courage and do the right thing? Yes. And when I did, God kept His promise.

I would have missed God's amazing intervening hand and my family would have missed His unique provision if we hadn't entered that trial. The *gift* was worth the *growth*. The *provision* was worth the *problem*. The *miracle* was worth the *madness*.

God is calling you forward in life. In some sense, He's calling you into pressure and problems. Embracing adult challenges is intimidating and scary, but it's worth it. God isn't merely leading you *to* trials, but *through* them! *Through* them is where His best blessings await. *Through* them is where His provision, His miracles, His amazing gifts abound. You must be willing to go *through* them so you can arrive on the other side where you will discover a lifetime of good gifts from God. You must be willing to embrace the pains of adulthood so God can bless and use you for the rest of your life. Which brings us to reward number two!

REWARD #2

THE TIMELESS GIFTS OF A GOOD LIFE

God's Word is filled with exceeding great and precious promises to the one who chooses to follow Him in life. He says in James 1:17, "Every good gift and every perfect gift is from above, and cometh down from the Father of lights, with whom is no variableness, neither shadow of turning." Again in Psalm 84:11 He says, "...the LORD will give grace and glory: no good thing will he withhold from them that walk uprightly." And He says, "Yea, the LORD shall give that which is good..." in Psalm 85:12.

God has a "warehouse-full" of good gifts and blessings that He plans to pour out upon you throughout the course of your life. It is His nature. He is a loving, giving, good God! Jesus said it this way, "If ye then, being evil, know how to give good gifts unto your children, how much more shall your Father which is in heaven give good things to them that ask him?" (Matthew 7:11). In other words, if an earthly father with a sinful nature has the capacity to give good gifts, how much more would a perfect, all-powerful Heavenly Father have that same desire and character!

You have a God that is prepared to mightily bless you as you *grow* into those blessings. You have a culture that is pulling you backward into immaturity. And you must make a choice—blessings or folly? Going forward is the tougher choice, but it has the greatest rewards!

Are you looking forward to the blessings yet? Embracing adulthood means that you embrace responsibility, pressure, stress, problems, and challenges. But it also means that you enjoy the rewards—and they are abundant and awesome! Please, trust me! You will be glad that you *endured* so that you could *enjoy* God's good gifts. "O taste and see that the LORD is good: blessed is the man that trusteth in him" (Psalm 34:8). "O LORD of hosts, blessed is the man that trusteth in thee" (Psalm 84:12).

Let's draw some conclusions from these biblical principles about God's desire to bless us:

***First, God delights in giving good gifts to His children.*** Please don't misunderstand. I'm not teaching a wealth and prosperity gospel. God is not our servant, and we're not to follow Him because of selfish desires. God doesn't bless those who artificially pursue Him to obtain *from* Him. He sees right through us, and He knows the deepest ambitions of our hearts. To pursue God as a *giver* is merely a pseudo-spiritual cover for pursuing things. We're not to pursue things; we're to pursue God—purely and sincerely.

God's Word teaches clearly that we're not to covet or pursue *things*. "No man that warreth entangleth himself with the affairs of this life; that he may please him who hath chosen him to be a soldier" (2 Timothy 2:4). "And he said unto them, Take heed, and beware of covetousness: for a man's life consisteth not in the abundance of the things which he possesseth" (Luke 12:15).

God's Word also teaches clearly that God *rewards* them that follow Him in truth. "…He is a rewarder of them that diligently seek him" (Hebrews 11:6). "The LORD recompense thy work, and a full reward be given thee of the LORD God of Israel, under whose wings thou art come to trust" (Ruth 2:12). "…And in keeping of them there is great reward" (Psalm 19:11). "…Thy Father, which seeth in secret, shall reward thee openly" (Matthew 6:18).

Our relationship with God is not about having a personal servant who will *do for* us and *give to* us. It is about having a personal Saviour and a Heavenly Father who loves us and provides for us. Don't crave things; crave *God*. As you do, you will discover a wonderful by-product—a God who delights in rewarding and blessing His children.

***Second, God's best gifts are intangible.*** If God called you on the phone and told you He would grant you one wish, what would it be? Would you ask for some object like a car, a house, or a large bank account? Or would you ask for something slightly less tangible but more valuable? Would you even consider asking Him to *favor* you?

There's an amazing word that God uses in Scripture in relating to His children. That word is *favour*, and it literally means "to look upon with graciousness and to bless with benefits, gifts, and pleasure." The most amazing thing is that God wants to give His favor to you! He plays favorites—

and you can be *His*! He gave it to Daniel—"Now God had brought Daniel into favour..." (Daniel 1:9). He gave it to Mary—"And the angel said unto her, Fear not, Mary: for thou hast found favour with God" (Luke 1:30). Jesus had it—"And Jesus increased in wisdom and stature, and in favour with God..." (Luke 2:52).

God's greatest gifts for your future are intangible. They aren't *things* but rather blessings—favor. Other than salvation, God's favor is perhaps the most wonderful gift you could have—the God of the universe reaching out of Heaven and intervening in your life in favorable ways—ways that bless you and those you love.

***Third, God's gifts follow maturity and faith.*** My daughter, Haylee, is incredible, but there are many things for which she is not ready. For instance, I would never give her a one-hundred-dollar bill and tell her to hold onto it for me. She's not ready for that responsibility. Now, I might give her a one-dollar bill. That's more in line with her level of maturity and responsibility.

Just a few days ago we purchased eyeglasses for her—to the tune of $150. Though she needs them, she's not ready to care for them. She's not ready for that level of responsibility, and so her mother and I have spent hours talking her through the details of caring for those expensive spectacles. To be honest, I'm scared to death that they won't last even to the end of this chapter!

In much the same way, God's blessings in your life will be commensurate with your maturity. He will only give you what you can handle. He will only give you bigger blessings when He knows that you are prepared for them. If you are a faithful steward in the little things, He will bless you with more. He will lead you through growing times to build you, stretch you, and strengthen you for bigger blessings in the future.

God calls you *through* growing up pressures so that you can fully enjoy and steward His better blessings and

His good gifts! If you want the better blessing, you must embrace the bitter growing pains. It's that simple.

God promised Abraham great blessing, but he first had to follow God in faith. God promised Moses that He would free the Israelites, but he first had to trust God through the plagues and pursuits of the Egyptians. God promised Joshua a land flowing with milk and honey, but he first had to cross the Jordan River and fight the enemies of God. God promised Mary and Joseph a Messiah, but they first had to embrace the scorn of an unbelieving culture. God promised David a kingdom, but he first had to face Goliath and then Saul's ruthless aggression. God promised Joseph a position of prominence and leadership, but he first had to endure rejection, slavery, and prison. God promised Paul a worldwide ministry, but he first had to endure prison, beatings, shipwrecks, and trials. God promised that His Son would be preeminent and receive all glory, but He first had to endure the shame of the Cross and the weight of our sin.

Throughout the Bible we see a God who leads us on a trail of trials to the pathway of blessings. That's how life works, by God's design.

Jesus is our first example in this principle. God's Word says, "Looking unto Jesus the author and finisher of our faith; who for the joy that was set before him endured the cross, despising the shame, and is set down at the right hand of the throne of God" (Hebrews 12:2).

Did you catch that? "...who for the joy that was set before him...." In other words, because of the reward and blessing that were set before Him, He "...endured the cross, despising the shame...." Jesus apparently found great joy in rescuing and saving you, so much so that He was willing to endure the Cross. Even so, if you will endure the pains and problems of embracing adulthood, you will be greatly delighted by the good gifts of God in your future! There is great joy set before you, if you will persist through the pressures.

Moses is another vivid example of this thinking, "Esteeming the reproach of Christ greater riches than the treasures in Egypt: for he had respect unto the recompence of the reward" (Hebrews 11:26). God called Moses to reject the rewards of Egypt, and fortunately, Moses could see the bigger picture. He knew there was a greater reward in following God, even into trials.

When I see your culture telling you to "stay young and stupid" for ten more years, it scares me for you! I see what your culture is turning down. They are walking away from big responsibilities and big blessings! I am experiencing amazing blessings in my own life that I would have completely missed if I had waited until my thirties to get serious about life. You can't waste time. You must seize the moment and move forward courageously. In so doing, the growing pains will prepare you for the blessings.

***Fourth, God will be better to you than you could be to yourself!*** Somehow, your generation has a mistaken image of God. The image is something of a twisted, distorted God who is determined to make you surrender, sacrifice, and suffer through life. Our picture of surrender is something close to Chinese water torture. Our picture of God's will is something like a POW camp. Our picture of ministry for Christ is something just above living in a cardboard box under an overpass.

We're convinced that God will not be as good to us as *we* would be to *ourselves*! Do you really think, for a second, that you could take better care of yourself than *God* can? Do you really think you're that much smarter, that much better, that much more generous and kind than your Creator? You couldn't be more wrong. You're nowhere close to God on this scale! You at your *kindest*, your *best*, couldn't touch the hem of God's garment of goodness and graciousness!

Let me share something that your generation has completely missed about God. He is extravagant, abundant, and exceedingly good! What suffering He calls you into will only produce greater blessing. What sacrifice He calls you to make will only lead to greater abundance. What surrender He leads you into will only give way to unsearchable treasure.

Surrendering to and following God is about as sacrificial as my kids getting into the car when I want to take them on a day trip. My kids know me. They trust me. They know what I mean when I say that I have a surprise planned. They don't worry, fear, and tremble. They anticipate! They get excited. They wake up early, get ready on their own, and are eager to go with me wherever I have planned! They ask, "Is it Disneyland? Are we going to the beach? Chuck E. Cheese? To the park to throw the football and feed the ducks? Are we going to shoot some rabbits?" Every mental image is positive, because they know my heart to bless them.

When God says "Surrender, submit, obey, follow me...," He's inviting you on an unthinkable, rewarding adventure with Him! Why do we assume He has negative plans? Why do we picture His will as being so "sacrificial" and "painful"? Because we don't know Him. We misjudge His heart. God's invitation ought to light us up on the inside! It should spark great delight, anticipation, and eagerness. Like a kid trying to get to sleep on Christmas Eve, we ought to be busting out of our "footy pajamas" to open the good gifts that God has in store for our future!

In 1 Timothy 6:17, God is the one who "...giveth us richly all things to enjoy." That verse doesn't only say He gives us "all things." It says He gives us all things "richly"! That's *extravagance*. Hebrews 10:35 says that our confidence or faith "...hath great recompence of reward." Not just a reward, not just a great reward, but a *great recompense* of *reward*. Let's break that down. If I told you that you would be rewarded for doing something, your expectations might be fairly low. If I said you would be greatly rewarded, your expectations might be higher. If I said, "You will have a great recompense of reward," now we're going somewhere! This is reward *cubed*! Sign me up!

God says, "But my God shall supply all your need according to his riches in glory by Christ Jesus" (Philippians 4:19). That verse doesn't say God will supply your need according to *your need*! It says He will supply your need "according to his riches"! There He goes again—*extravagance*! God doesn't "just barely" provide; He *abundantly* provides. He doesn't "barely satisfy"—He *abundantly* satisfies. "They shall be abundantly satisfied with the fatness of thy house; and thou shalt make them drink of the river of thy pleasures" (Psalm 36:8). He doesn't half-fill your life glass; He overflows it!

Jesus said, "For all these things do the nations of the world seek after: and your Father knoweth that ye have need of these things. But rather seek ye the kingdom of God; and all these things shall be added unto you" (Luke 12:30–31). In other words, seek God and He'll take care of everything else, because He's in the giving business!

I want to let you in on a HUGE secret that your culture just doesn't get. God is in the business of *exceeding* your expectations! He is in the business of *majorly* fulfilling your heart's desires and your deepest longings. But He has some conditions. You must surrender your desires and pursue Him with all of your heart. You must love Him above all. I know it seems like sacrifice for the moment, but in the end you sacrificed nothing and gained everything! You can't afford to pass this up!

> *God is in the business of exceeding your expectations.*

God is *extravagant*—and those who love Him fully experience that extravagance firsthand. I could write pages about the countless ways that God has abundantly fulfilled the desires of my heart. My whole life is a delightful surprise to me! God has been far better to me than I ever could have been to myself! I can't believe that God allows me the privileges, the opportunities, and the incredible blessings He has given. It is overwhelming, and every day His mercies are new and His blessings seem greater.

I think He says it best this way, "Now unto him that is able to do exceeding abundantly above all that we ask or think, according to the power that worketh in us" (Ephesians 3:20). You can't even begin to comprehend how God desires to exceed your expectations if you will give Him the chance.

There's one more gigantic truth I want you to embrace as we wrap up these thoughts about God's timeless gifts.

## God's Gifts Hold the Most Significance

You've probably never thought of this, so stay with me for a moment. The significance of a gift is not determined by the gift—it is determined by the *giver*. Don't let that get by you—think about it. The value or the power of a gift is determined by the one who gave it to you. Let me illustrate.

When Dana and I were falling in love, we made it a regular habit to give each other gifts. We dated for three years before our wedding day, and throughout those years we were deeply, madly in love with each other—so much so that we were obsessed with giving things to each other. Sometimes those gifts cost a lot of money and sometimes they cost nothing. For instance, for a birthday one year she gave me a $100 leather jacket, but for our fifteen-month-twenty-two day anniversary of our dating relationship she gave me a note with little red hearts and perfume all over it. For Valentine's Day I gave her a fairly inexpensive bracelet, but the day we got engaged I gave a fairly expensive ring.

You're really going to think we're nuts when I tell you this. We saved things from each other that would have been trash to any mentally stable person. When we shared a McDonald's hot fudge sundae, she saved the spoon! When I gave her a Tootsie Roll Pop, she saved the wrapper! When I colored her a special Easter egg—yes, she saved it—for years!

(Yuck!) When we took walks on the beach, she would hand me a piece of driftwood, and I'd save it. To this very day, we have large boxes in our garage filled with things we gave each other. All these years later, they still mean something. To the rest of the world, they are trash, but to us they are important symbols of a highly valuable, loving relationship that has existed now for twenty years.

In every case, these gifts mean something because of the giver. The significance of the engagement ring was not the ring, but the love and the giver behind the ring. The significance of a Tootsie Roll wrapper was not the candy itself, but the giver and the relationship represented behind it! You see, the giver gives significance to all gifts—both great and small. When you're in love with the giver, even little gifts are highly valuable!

Now, how does this truth play out in your future with God?

***First, when you are your own giver, things mean nothing.*** What if your parents approached you on your next birthday and said, "We love you, but we want you to go buy your own gifts." First, it would probably hurt you. Second, you might enjoy the shopping and the buying, but the gifts will be lacking something—significance. They won't be special. When you buy *yourself* something, it means less than if someone you love purchased it for you.

Now I realize that every good gift is from God, but when you venture into life without Him, you don't see them that way. When you walk away from God, you sort of take life into your own hands. You see yourself as your own provider. Can you do okay? Sure, for a while. God isn't trying to squash you. He will still provide for you and even allow you to take the credit for it sometimes. You could probably get a good job, buy a nice car, have nice things, and even eventually have a nice house. But there's a major problem—no *significance*. Things have no value to the heart when they aren't attached to a loving giver.

When you see these things as gifts to yourself, they lose their luster rather quickly. The happiness wears off, the things don't mean much, and you must continue on your endless search for heart satisfaction. You see, though you are good to yourself, it won't mean much! And no matter how good you are—no matter how nice the things you accumulate—you will still be empty inside. You'll be like a man who bought his own wedding ring—no fiancé, no love, no future family in view—just a pointless ring—a ring that serves as a constant reminder of what's missing. Even so, when you accumulate *things* with no giver, they only serve to remind you that you're still missing something (someone) very special!

No girl wants an engagement ring without a guy attached! No man wants a bridal gown without a bride inside! Even so, gifts without God attached mean nothing. No *thing* has true value apart from a loving Heavenly Father who gave it!

***Second, when God is the giver, everything means something special!*** Let's flip this equation around for a moment.

It's only when *things* come from God that *things* have any value! And when you know that the things you have are *from* God, then *everything* becomes highly valuable and special! When they are from God, even *small* things add great joy and blessedness to your heart over and over again. And the big gifts—like a car, a home, a child, a spouse—are beyond belief, way over the top, massive in their value. Here's the really cool part. God's gifts don't lose their significance over time.

When you buy yourself a car, it will really be a wonderful experience for about two weeks! But eventually the significance will wear off and then it's just a car and a payment! Eventually you'll have a "ho-hum" attitude and the value of the gift will become less significant to your heart. But when God gives you a car—when you see your purchase as a direct gift enabled and provided by God—it will *never* lose its significance! Even temporary things when given by God have an eternal "special-ness"!

Even little things that most people lose interest in will continue to delight your heart over and over again—because God's thumbprint is on them! It becomes highly special because it was a gift from your Father in Heaven!

We have an annual Resurrection Sunday tradition at our house. We color eggs during a family night, and then my wife and I develop a little treasure hunt around the house. She purchases some plastic eggs and we stuff them with silly little things—candy, coins, love notes, etc. Then we create clues and hide the real and the plastic eggs all over the house. It doesn't take long and the gifts are relatively insignificant and affordable—stuff like, "a picnic at the park with Mom and Dad."

Well, you would think that we give these children the world! The anticipation that builds, the excitement of the hunt, and the delight that is expressed over every candy, every coin, and every note is purely indescribable. This is a major "delight" event at the Schmidt house! Hearts are greatly blessed by this hunt. This ranks right up there with family vacation and a day at Disneyland in my kids' minds.

Why? Do they crave marshmallow bunnies and quarters that much? Do these things really make that big of a difference in their lives? No. They love being loved! They love knowing that my wife and I put the time, planning, and effort into treating them so special. Their hearts bask in the love more than their wallets bask in the abundance!

The plastic eggs, the notes, the coins, and the candy would be meaningless if we just piled it all on the counter and left the kids at home alone for the day. Yet, our presence and our expressions of love make even the smallest piece of plastic a treasure to the heart!

That's how your life with God will be if you go forward with God. Every small gift, every little detail—things that most people completely pass up—will mean the world to you! Your heart will be delighted day after day after day! You will be speechless and overwhelmed by God's exceeding goodness to you. Small stuff that would normally mean nothing will suddenly be "out of this world" special! Big stuff will be unspeakably overwhelming! You will venture into each new day like a kid on Christmas morning, and even the smallest things will fill your heart with blessedness— sacred delight.

While the world "ho-hums" along, searching and longing for that sacred delight—that overwhelming, heart-level happiness—you'll be fully immersed in a river of delight from your Heavenly Father! You'll be constantly swept downstream in the abundant flow of His blessings. You'll discover what God means when He says, "...good measure, pressed down, and shaken together, and running over..." (Luke 6:38). You'll experience firsthand what Jesus means when He says, "...I am come that they might have life, and that they might have it more abundantly" (John 10:10).

When you are your own giver, *things* mean *nothing*. The heart stays empty. But when God is your giver, *everything* suddenly means *something* special! What a great way to live life!

What a great God we have! He specializes in exceeding our expectations. He not only made your heart, but also your desires and dreams, and He plans to spend the rest of your life providing for you and blessing you with good gifts! He is *extravagant*. He will be exceedingly better to you than *you* would be to *yourself*!

He does have some conditions—love Him first and foremost. Surrender and obey Him. Follow Him with your whole heart. Pursue Him and walk with Him—nothing hard, just basic biblical living.

There is unspeakable joy and delight found in receiving a lifetime of good gifts from your Heavenly Father. From His hand, every good gift is highly special and significant.

Without Him, even really great gifts end up empty and pointless.

Do you get jittery when you hear the words surrender, follow, obey God? Why? Why not be like my kids when I say, "Hop in the car, we're going someplace special!" Trust Him. He's taking you someplace special! Now, get in the car, buckle up, trust your God, and get ready for a great time!

> *But as it is written, Eye hath not seen, nor ear heard, neither have entered into the heart of man, the things which God hath prepared for them that love him.*
>
> —1 CORINTHIANS 2:9

# CHAPTER SEVEN

## ONE RED PAPER CLIP, PLEASE...

*Reward #3—The Eternal Rewards of a Faithful Steward*

Many of today's young adults spend a good portion of their lives disappointed and "starting over." At eighteen, many enter college, work through four to six years of school only to owe an enormous amount of money and discover that they weren't as prepared for real life as their college led them to believe. Disappointment increases when they discover they can't get the "job of their dreams" and have to settle for whatever pays the bills— waiting tables, bagging groceries, working a checkout line. In time, the degree usually helps them obtain something close to what they had hoped for, but disappointment returns as they discover they don't really *want* to do this job that they so long dreamed about.

So, they move on, find another opportunity, and *start over*. In a matter of months, the delight of the new job fades, the new scenery blends into the background, and life becomes drab and disappointing once again. They try a new relationship, a new hangout, a new set of friends only to find out the new friends are as disappointed and confused as they are. Several years out of college, and still in student loan debt, they look for another opportunity to *start over*.

They rush into another move, another job, another relationship, maybe even a marriage and a family—all the while looking for happiness of heart that only God can give. It's all decided so emotionally and haphazardly. It is, at best, *guesswork*. Still, in a matter of time, this third job, fourth relationship, and even the marriage and family loses its luster. Disillusionment, disappointment, and even despair set in. Soon a divorce is inevitable and the precious hearts of little children are pulled into the bloody fray of misguided adult decisions. They never recover, but at least misguided mom or duped dad gets to *start over* again and take their next blind leap in their ongoing search for significance.

And to think, these people think *we* are weird for living God's way! Amazing.

In the TIME article that I quoted earlier, Jeffrey Arnett, a developmental psychologist at Clarks University, actually believes that the twixter way of living life is a good thing. He believes that your generation is preparing for adulthood. I beg to differ on this point. It's not preparing—it's postponing! Since when do you prepare for something by ignoring it?

He states, "This is the one time of their lives when they're not responsible for anyone else or to anyone else, so they have this wonderful freedom to really focus on their own lives and work on becoming the kind of person they want to be." The article continues, "In his view, what looks like incessant, hedonistic play is the twixters' way of trying on jobs and partners and personalities and making sure that when they do settle down, they do it the right way, their way."

I want to climb into your head right now, knock on your brain, and shout to you, "This is the *wrong* way not the *right* way!" When you live life "your way," you will be continually and sorely disappointed. *Your* way is the wrong way. *Your* way will lead you to misery. Life isn't about you, and your life is not your own. "What? know ye not that your body is the temple of the Holy Ghost which is in you, which ye have of God, and ye are not your own? For ye are bought with a price: therefore glorify God in your body, and in your spirit, which are God's" (1 Corinthians 6:19–20). The sooner you embrace this truth, the sooner you can really begin living, and the better your life will be!

## College Isn't the Cure All

Somewhere along the line, my generation and my parents' generation handed off the baton of preparing you for life. For the most part, we handed that baton to the colleges of America. The sad news is, *they've failed—royally*!

TIME says it this way, "Matt Swann, 27, says, 'Kids used to go to college to get educated. That's what I did, which I think now was a bit naive. Being smart after college doesn't really mean anything.'

"College is the institution most of us entrust to watch over the transition to adulthood, but somewhere along the line that transition has slowed to a crawl. In a TIME poll of people ages 18 to 29, only 32% of those who attended college left school by age 21. In fact, the average college student takes five years to finish. The era of the four-year college degree is all but over.

"Most colleges are seriously out of step with the real world in getting students ready to become workers in the post college world. More traditional schools are scrambling to give their courses a practical spin. As colleges struggle to get their students ready for real-world jobs, they are charging more for what they deliver.

"The resulting debt is a major factor in keeping twixters from moving on and growing up. Meanwhile, those expensive, time-sucking college diplomas have become worth less than ever. So many more people go to college now—a 53% increase since 1970—that the value of a degree on the job market has been diluted. The advantage in wages for college-degree holders hasn't risen significantly since the late 1990s, according to the Bureau of Labor Statistics.

"To compensate, a lot of twixters go back to school for graduate and professional degrees. But piling on extra degrees costs precious time and money and pushes adulthood even further into the future."

The November 13, 2006 issue of *Newsweek* magazine included an article by a disillusioned young lady who stated the following about the discrepancy between her college education and her real-world life: "My friends and I are graduates of Wesleyan, Barnard, Stanford and Yale. We've earned 3.9 GPAs and won academic awards. Yet none of us knows what a Roth IRA is or can master a basic tax form. And heaven help us when April comes and we have to file tax returns.... There's a discrepancy between what we learn in school and what we need to know for work, and there must be some way for universities to bridge this gap.... How about a class on renting an apartment?

"...College students are graduating with greater debt than ever before, yet we haven't learned how to manage our money. We can wing it for only so long before employers start wising up to our real-world incompetence. In fact, they already are: a study released last month showed that hundreds of employers have found their college-graduate hires to be 'woefully unprepared' for the job market.... All this raises a disturbing question: when I spent a ton of time and money on my fancy degree, what exactly was I buying?"

Do you see the life trap that this culture has created for you? You've been taught that college will prepare you, but six years later you discover it didn't, so you search for other answers. You've been taught that a college education will support you, but later, you find out otherwise, so you search for other solutions. Fifteen years out of high school, you're still trying to figure it out, and you're still paying off your student loans! Don't live this life!

Now, I'm not saying don't go to college. I'm just trying to show you the truth—college isn't the cure-all. Secular college isn't all that culture tells you it is. College alone doesn't get you ready for adulthood. If anything, it postpones adulthood by loading you with debt and a false sense of maturity. Many people are graduating from college as educated fools—no wisdom, no understanding, no direction, no purpose, no God.

It's time for a major philosophy change in your heart. Here it is; buckle up—this is the heart of this chapter.

You don't go to college to get ready for life. You embrace life to get ready for eternity! Adulthood is not a destination. It is a preparation phase for something much, much bigger and much better! See the bigger picture. Look beyond life for a moment.

My daughter has a real problem. Her six-year-old head is the exact height of most side mirrors on car doors. Her height isn't the problem though. Walking with her head down in parking lots is the problem. This kid, as precious as she is, just doesn't get it about car mirrors. On many trips to Wal-Mart, Target, or the grocery store, she whacks her head on a car mirror. She's usually deep in thought or transfixed by some toy, not looking up, and SMACK, another welt, another cry session. You would think after about fifty times, she would remember—mirrors, look out for mirrors—but no. The other day she was walking between two cars, smacked her head on one, grabbed her head, yelled out, spun around, and smacked the back of her head on another! It happened so fast she didn't know what hit her. It's hard to laugh and be sympathetic at the same time, but I try. I'm going to buy her a motorcycle helmet pretty soon!

This is what your culture is doing: walking through life with their heads down—SMACK. And they aren't learning the lesson. Every few years they smash their lives into another series of bad decisions! Stop walking with your head down—life is much bigger than this moment. Life is bigger than the next five or ten years. Life is bigger than your lifetime. Life is about *eternity*, and it's time that you understand the reward of living with your head up, looking far forward.

REWARD #3
THE ETERNAL REWARDS OF A FAITHFUL STEWARD

We saw two chapters ago the first reward of embracing life—eternal significance in God's plan. Then we saw the second reward—the timeless gifts of a good life. While these first two relate more to time itself, this third reward is bigger. It will require you to lift your head and look into eternity. It is determined *now*, but won't be had until *Heaven*. What do I mean? Let's find out.

## God's Excessive Goodness Just Keeps on Going

Have you ever wondered why God offers to save you? Honestly, He could have just obliterated us and started over. Why did He keep us? Why do we even matter to Him?

This is a big question, and even the Apostle Paul said it was a mystery. Yet, there are several incredible passages of Scripture that crack the door of reasoning slightly and let a little light through on this subject. One of my favorites is Ephesians 2:4–7.

> But God, who is rich in mercy, for his great love wherewith he loved us, Even when we were dead in sins, hath quickened us together with Christ, (by grace ye are saved;) And hath raised us up together, and made us sit together in heavenly places in Christ Jesus: That in the

ages to come he might shew the exceeding riches of his
grace in his kindness toward us through Christ Jesus.

The first two verses of that passage tell us *what* God did
for us—He loved us, quickened us (or made us alive again),
raised us up, and gave us a heavenly place with Jesus Christ.
But then that next verse takes the cake by telling us *why*—
"That in the ages to come he might shew the exceeding
riches of his grace in his kindness toward us through Christ
Jesus." I don't know if we can conquer this massive truth,
but let's try.

"That in the ages to come..."—it's all about what's
coming after this life! We are living in this age, but there
are *ages to come*. This word *ages* is where we get our English
word *eon* which means "a length of time too long to
measure." Whoa! That's big. God saved us and quickened us
so that He could spend *more time than can be measured* doing
something. What?

"That...he might shew the exceeding riches of his grace
in his kindness toward us...." God's riches and kindness
are unsearchable, unimaginable, limitless. He exceeds all
human understanding in greatness and goodness. And for
some mysterious reason, He has planned to spend the ages
to come—eons—doing one thing—"shewing" or expressing
that kindness and those riches toward *you*. Do you get it?
For no explainable reason, at least to the human mind,
God has an eternal Christmas morning planned in Heaven
for you. This is better than every birthday party, every
Christmas, and every special event of your life all wrapped
up together. Nothing can come close to this. You've never
experienced love, goodness, kindness, and riches on this
level. You don't even have the mental capacity to think of
it. It defies description. It cannot be comprehended. This is
God's super-abundant, gigantically good heart being poured
out upon you for eons to come!

Wow! If God and eternity are that good, then I'm glad
I'm not my own! I'm glad life is about more than going to

college, getting a job, and starting over, and over…and over. More importantly, in light of this vast goodness in the ages to come, how do I prepare? What must I do to get ready for the "ages to come"?

Well, you don't sit back and ignore life. You don't walk through life with your head down. God makes it clear that your vapor—your life—matters in the ages to come. What you do in *this* life matters in the *next*—in more ways than one. The decisions you make now have a major impact on the rewards you enjoy then, and understanding the bigger picture will cause you to do a couple things.

*First, you will anticipate eternity.* I meet a lot of young adults who dread the thought of Jesus coming back. They dread the thought of dying and going to Heaven. They'd rather have a root canal. The unknown, the mystery scares them. How silly! This is worse than dreading your wedding reception! This isn't something you dread—it's something you anticipate!

*Second, you will get serious about living life correctly now so that you can please God!* You will want your life to honor the God who has shown you such exceeding goodness. You don't receive such endless kindness and spit on it. You don't take salvation and run away. You don't anticipate heavenly places with Christ and tell Him to stay out of your life until then! Seeing His endless, eternal goodness should compel you to embrace life courageously in faith and to live it to the utmost for Him. It's all about *Him*!

## The Stewardship of Life

In order to understand the eternal rewards of a faithful steward, let's talk about the stewardship. A steward is someone who manages the property, finances, or household of another. The biblical principle at the foundation of this reward is that you are the steward of God. Your life and everything you have is from Him, and He requires that you steward, or manage it wisely, productively, and faithfully. It's all on loan from God. One day you will return it to Him with interest, and He's expecting you to have done something fruitful and profitable with it.

In 2005, twenty-six-year-old Kyle McDonald had a dream. He wanted to own a house, but he had no way of purchasing that house. In fact, Kyle didn't have much at all. He lived in an apartment, did odd jobs to pay the bills, and dreamed of becoming a writer. Rather than bemoan what he didn't have, he decided to embrace what he did have and to do the best he could with it. So, he got creative.

Enter the red paper clip. Kyle had one red paper clip and an ingenious idea. Maybe, just maybe he could invest that paper clip and in time turn it into a house. Stupid? Impossible? We'll see.

Kyle listed his red paper clip on a trading website and asked for anything better in exchange for it. Somehow, someone saw Kyle's offer and traded him a fish-shaped pen for that one red paper clip. He then listed the fish-shaped pen and traded that for a ceramic knob. The knob traded for a camping stove, which in turn traded for a generator. A few trades later, Kyle had gone through a snow mobile, a trip to the Canadian Rockies, a supply truck, and a recording contract. It's hard to believe, but by April of 2006, Kyle had gained a full year's rent in Phoenix, Arizona.

By this time, the internet and the news media had picked up on Kyle's quest and were following it carefully. He became a guest of nationwide talk shows and news specials; he was written about in periodicals and newspapers, and he made dozens of media appearances. In the process of it all, a movie producer picked up on his story and offered a paid movie role in his trade adventure.

You wouldn't have guessed it, but about a year from the listing of his original red paper clip, Kyle was offered a $45,000, three-bedroom, 1,100 square-foot house in the city of Kipling, Saskatchewan, Canada as a trade for the movie role. He had actually pulled it off. In less than a year, Kyle turned a red paper clip into a $45,000 property. That's a pretty healthy return on an investment.

You might be wondering what you have to offer God—why He would consider you so *valuable*? You might have reasoned that your life, in the big picture, amounts to about as much as that one red paper clip. From our perspective, in the light of God's greatness, that's about all we have to offer. But God has a different perspective.

A "red paper clip" can change the universe when it's in the hands of Almighty God! Moses gave God a wooden rod, and He changed a nation. David gave God a poetic heart and sling, and God freed a nation and established His throne forever. A lad gave God some loaves and fishes, and He fed a multitude. A widow gave God her last meal, and He sustained her life. Namaan gave God seven dips in muddy water, and He healed a deadly disease. Gideon gave God three hundred men, and God defeated a massive army. Joseph gave God his dreams, and God let him rule a nation. Daniel gave God an excellent spirit, and God favored him above all the princes. Rahab gave God a scarlet thread, and He gave her forgiveness and salvation. Peter gave Jesus a feisty attitude and a fishing boat, and Jesus gave him a ton of fish and a calling to change the world. Paul gave God a wretched past, and God used him to reach the world. Mary Magdalene gave Jesus some precious ointment, and God filled her heart with Himself.

What do you have to give God? What are you doing with it? What will you have to show for it when you meet Him face to face? This is the "trade of the centuries"! God is looking for your "one red paper clip" and, in exchange, you get everything that He is and everything He desires to do through you!

You see, when God formed your "paper-clip" of a life, He instilled the seeds of eternal value into you. They are but seeds mind you, but seeds can bear a profound harvest if they are given to God and stewarded properly. You must yield those seeds back to God, plant them in the field of His will, and nurture them to maturity by His grace. When God created you, He gave you *potential*—the raw abilities to impact the universe. He gave you the possibility of becoming someone very special and intricately meaningful to His eternal purpose. In other words, your "paper clip" is eternally valuable to your Creator, but without Him, it's just a paper clip. Wouldn't you like to know, for all of eternity, that your life *mattered*? Wouldn't you like to hear God's voice say, "Well done"?

## Jesus Illustrates Life Stewardship

In Matthew 25:14-34, Jesus taught a parable about a wealthy man who was taking a trip. Before he left, he divided his money among his servants. To one he gave five talents, to another two, and to another one—"to every man according to his several ability." Immediately after the man left town, the first servant took his five talents and stepped out on a limb. He got risky in a good way. He invested the talents and doubled them to ten talents. The second servant did the same and turned two talents into four. But the third servant got scared. He was a twixter! He didn't want to grow up, take risks, and stick his neck out. He preferred to stay home, play video games, and vegetate. He chose to dig a hole and bury his talent. The Bible says he "hid his lord's money."

After a long time, the wealthy man returned home to reckon with his servants. The word *reckon* means "to take account of or to compute." This man *expected* a return. He wanted what was rightfully his, but he wanted to see it multiplied. And as you might expect, he was very pleased with the first two servants. To both servants he said, "Well done, thou good and faithful servant: thou hast been faithful over a few things, I will make thee ruler over many things: enter thou into the joy of thy lord."

The third servant didn't fare so well. This guy was a *real winner*. He probably hated to put his video game on pause long enough to report back to his master. When asked about the one talent, he started fumbling and stuttering a lame excuse about how "hard" his master was and how shrewd he was. Again, this guy apparently lost a few of his marbles somewhere along the way—probably buried them with his talent. (For future reference, don't ever make excuses for *yourself* by insulting your *employer*—unless you just hate your job.)

Too much in a hurry to get back to his nothing life, this servant casually dismisses his mismanagement, blames his hard-nosed boss, and gives the one talent back. What a loser! During the time his boss was absent, the sum total of his effort was to hide the one thing he was given to do. Then, he apparently sat around watching Dish Network, eating Ding Dongs, and snoring his trivial life into oblivion. In the end, he was a total zero—nothing to show. If you had to prove this guy's value in a court of law, there would have been no evidence. He was probably the brother-in-law of the foreman on the job—otherwise he would have never been hired!

I wish I could see a picture of his face when his boss responded to his pathetic existence. "Thou wicked and slothful servant...Thou oughtest therefore to have put my money to the exchangers, and then at my coming I should have received mine own with usury." Wicked and slothful—those are strong words. Some wouldn't appreciate God calling twixters "wicked and slothful." Back off, God—they're just irresponsibly exploring their options! In God's economy, when you bury your potential, you are wicked and slothful. That sort of smacks you in the face if you think about it. Just the kind of "jolt" many in this generation need.

From there, the lord takes the one talent from the loser and gives it to the ten-talent servant. What a slap in the face! If that's not politically incorrect, I don't know what would be. Talk about robbing the poor to pay the rich! Then he proceeds to instruct his servants in "Life Stewardship 101"—those who do good with what they have will be given a lot more; those who bury what they have will lose it all. And in the end, he toasts the loser—literally! I'm talking flames and smoke. Now you know where we get the saying "you're fired."

Then, Jesus turns the story in a direction that most people don't consider. His very next words are, "When the Son of man shall come in his glory, and all the holy angels with him, then shall he sit upon the throne of his glory: And before him shall be gathered all nations: and he shall separate them one from another, as a shepherd divideth his sheep from the goats: And he shall set the sheep on his right hand, but the goats on the left. Then shall the King say unto them on his right hand, Come, ye blessed of my Father, inherit the kingdom prepared for you from the foundation of the world" (Matthew 25:31–34).

Thank you, Lord, for allowing me to be a sheep! Jesus turns the whole story on edge by taking you to the end of earthly time when His faithful stewards will inherit His eternal kingdom. He calls us His sheep, and He says we are "blessed of my Father." Wow! That's a heart-full!

## The Parable Applied

The lessons we must take away from such a story are many. We are the servants. God has given you "talents"—and we're not talking merely about singing-and-dancing kind of talents. In this story the "talents" represent your potential—all the raw abilities, gifts, interests, and unique qualities that He placed in you. He has matched your talents with your ability and He knows exactly what you are capable of by His grace. He has given you a vapor of time. He's given you a red paper clip packed with explosive power, and He's expecting you to invest, multiply, and return it to Him with added value. He's coming back soon. You will one day bow before Him and reckon with Him. You will give account personally for everything that He has entrusted to you. With this in mind, you must do several things.

***First, you must discover your gifts.*** Perhaps you already have discovered your gifts, or perhaps you've spent too much time in front of the TV. You are packed with gifts that God has given to you—spiritual gifts, natural abilities, unique personality traits, and raw potential. If you don't know what they are, then this is where you must start. There's not time to go into each spiritual gift, but suffice it to say that there are many, and you probably have more than one! You must uncover those gifts and abilities. They are intricately tied to your destiny and your unique identity in God's purpose and plan.

***Second, you must develop your gifts.*** You must take the seeds that God has given you and grow them into fruit-bearing abilities for His glory. You can't bury your gifts. That's what the twixters are doing! You must take what God has given you and grow it, expand it, multiply it.

If you can sing, develop your voice. If you can teach, learn how to teach powerfully. If you can lead, become a dynamic servant leader. If you can administrate details, then expand that ability. If you can handle numbers, then become an expert. If you can sympathize with the hurting, then take it to the next level. You're never more uniquely you and more honoring to God than when you put the remote control down and develop what God placed in you. These are God-given gifts and you will answer to Him for what you've done with them. Take these abilities to school and make them better than you ever thought they could be!

***Third, you must deploy your gifts.*** This is where life goes to the next level altogether! It's "over-the-top" fun to take God-given abilities—things that God made you good at—and use them for eternal purposes to His glory. Put those talents to the exchangers—get them into the open market! Uncover them and put them into use. Sing. Teach. Lead. Encourage. Sympathize. Calculate. Build. Design. Create. Write. Play. Do what God made you to do, and do it for Him. Once you've found those God-given abilities, live them out. Do them.

While every other twixter in the world is "starting over" with the next job, the next partner, the next "buzz"—live out your unique potential to the glory of your Heavenly Father. Be a faithful steward while the Lord has taken His journey. Turn the TV off. Put the PlayStation away. Break off the bad relationship. Forsake the wickedness of the world. Turn away from folly. Embrace life! Embrace God! Embrace your potential and partner with the Lord of the universe in being a productive, fruitful, growing, multiplying steward of all the good talents He has given to you. This is real living!

If you have no clue what I'm talking about—no clue what you should be doing for God or what your purpose is, then I would encourage you to read *Discover Your Destiny*—a book the Lord allowed me to write a few years ago. I can't take the time to develop the thought, but the journey is worth the discovery!

Don't sit around and wait for destiny to hit you on the head—it never will. God opens doors to those who are already *in motion*! Get in motion! Put your gifts into play—in your job, your church, your home, and your community. Begin serving God *somehow—now*. Invest your life into the eternal cause of Christ and watch how God will open doors, lead you to opportunities, and expand your abilities and privileges.

As a side note, when I say "deploy" your gifts, I mean "for God"—and there's no greater way to serve God than in a local church. God is clear in His Word that the local church is the place where every Christian should establish himself in growing in grace, discovering his spiritual gifts, and deploying them for the service of Christ. Jesus loved the church so much that He died for it! You can't possibly discover your God-given potential without becoming an integral part of a Bible-believing church family. I challenge you to find the Bible-believing local church where God desires to use you, commit yourself to His plan, and use your unique gifts for His glory in that place.

## The Soon Coming Reward Ceremony

Why does all this matter? And how does it relate to the eternal rewards of a faithful steward? It's all in the *reckoning*. One day you will bow before your Creator and give account. This isn't something of which to be terrified, unless you're an unjust steward. This is a reward ceremony for those who faithfully steward their "vapor."

Second Corinthians 5:9–10 teaches us this: "Wherefore we labour, that, whether present or absent, we may be accepted of him. For we must all appear before the judgment seat of Christ; that every one may receive the things done in his body, according to that he hath done, whether it be good or bad." Paul said, this is why I'm laboring—to be accepted of Him. I want to honor my Master. I want to present Him a life well lived. I want to give Him back an invested life that grew and multiplied.

In 1 Corinthians 3:12–14, we get a clear picture of this accounting time: "Now if any man build upon this foundation gold, silver, precious stones, wood, hay, stubble; Every man's work shall be made manifest: for the day shall declare it, because it shall be revealed by fire; and the fire shall try every man's work of what sort it is. If any man's work abide which he hath built thereupon, he shall receive a reward."

Stubble or precious stones—that's what your paper clip will amount to when you stand before Christ—depending on what you did with it. In that moment, you will fully recognize, for the first time, exactly who you are, who God is, and how massively good He has been to you. "For now we see through a glass, darkly; but then face to face: now I know in part; but then shall I know even as also I am known" (1 Corinthians 13:12). The gray areas will suddenly be crystal clear, and the truth will be fully known.

Then, every choice or non-choice, every decision or indecision, every moment of every day, every motive, every desire, every thought, every deed will be tried by fire. The eyes of God will personally inspect your life-investment. He is looking to reward you and to applaud you into His blessed, abundant favor. Your every sense will be awakened, every nerve alert, every breath suspenseful as there before your eyes are the nail-pierced hands that you so often heard about—the all-powerful, Great Shepherd of the sheep who gave His life for you. You will bow in humble reverence. You will immediately wish you had given Him more—that you had sacrificed more cheerfully, surrendered more willingly, and served more faithfully.

If you are saved, you will enter into His rest regardless of what's left of your life. God's heart would rather applaud you into His presence, but if necessary, He will assist you into His presence by wiping the tears of regret from your eyes. After the smoke clears, only that which you did for God will remain—gold, silver, and precious stones.

Both scenarios are found in God's Word. In Acts 7, the faithful deacon Stephen was stoned for preaching Christ. Just before he died, God opened his eyes to an astounding sight—Jesus standing at the Father's right hand and looking on. Stephen's words were, "Behold, I see the heavens opened, and the Son of man standing on the right hand of God"—a standing ovation from the King of Heaven as He rises to

His feet and boldly proclaims, "Well done, thou good and faithful servant."

Yet, in Revelation 21 we find another scenario—"And God shall wipe away all tears from their eyes; and there shall be no more death, neither sorrow, nor crying, neither shall there be any more pain: for the former things are passed away" (Revelation 21:4).

What a gracious God—no matter what the fire of His judgment reveals, He will wrap you up in His arms and welcome you home as His child.

The twixter article states, "To [emerging adults] the period from eighteen to twenty-five is a kind of sandbox, a chance to build castles and knock them down, experiment with different careers, knowing that none of it really counts." While it might be nice if that were true, I have great news for you. It *isn't*. *All* of it *counts*—every moment of every day. Get out of the sandbox and get on with developing and deploying your unique potential for God!

In closing, let me pose one question that is worthy of much consideration—would you rather present a well-stewarded life and enter Heaven to God's smile and "Well done," or present knocked-down sandcastles mixed with wood, hay and stubble and have Him wipe away the stinging tears of regret?

It's up to you, but as for me, I'm aiming for "Well done."

## CHAPTER EIGHT

# SURF'S UP OLD DUDE

*Turning the Corner and Getting on Track*

To culture, you are a thing to study—an anomaly to understand. To God, you are a precious child on a significant life quest of eternal proportions. Culture will abuse you, drain you, and dispense of you. God will nurture you, guide you, and provide for you. Culture will confuse you. God will use you for His glory. It doesn't take a rocket scientist to choose God.

The twixter article puts young adults in a unique market category and claims that marketing specialists have a legitimate financial interest in keeping them ignorant and dependent upon parents. Try this on for size, "Marketers have picked up on the fact that twixters on their personal voyages of discovery tend to buy lots of stuff along the way. 'They are the optimum market to be going after for consumer electronics,' says David Morrison, president of Twentysomething Inc., a marketing consultancy based in Philadelphia. 'Most of their needs are taken care of by Mom and Dad, so their income is largely discretionary. [Many] are living at home [with] flat-screen TVs in their bedrooms and brand new cars in the driveway.' Some twixters may want to grow up, but corporations and advertisers have a real stake in keeping them in a tractable, exploitable, pre-adult state—living at home, spending their money on toys."

If you are twenty-something, you are a marketing statistic—exploitable, tractable (very easy to control or persuade). Doesn't that just make you feel warm and fuzzy and special all over?! Actually, it should fire you up! I pray it lights a passion within you to reject this deceptive culture and embrace God's purpose with fresh energy and vision. You are more than a marketing statistic to God. He isn't exploiting you.

TIME quotes writer and director, Zach Braff saying, "In the past, people got married and got a job and had kids, but now there's a new ten years that people are using to try and find out what kind of life they want to lead. For a lot of people, the weight of all the possibility is overwhelming."

The following quotes epitomize the sum total of the world's solutions for your generation:

"…Most of the problems that twixters face are hard to see, and that makes it harder to help them."

"There are few road maps in the popular culture…to get twixters where they need to go."

What a blessing!

Let's draw some conclusions on exactly where we stand before we move on to part three of this book.

First, we've seen the root problems of immaturity, irresponsibility, ignorance, rebellion, and folly. We've taken a good hard look at what's really holding you back spiritually. It's not culture, college, or clinical psychology—it's folly—foolishness in the heart and fear of the future.

Second, we've taken three chapters to explore the amazing rewards of strapping on your boots and going forward into life with God. The first reward is a life of eternal significance because you matter to God. The second is a good life filled with deeply meaningful gifts from your Heavenly Father. And just when you think it can't get any better, the third is the eternal rewards of a faithful steward— being able to see gold and silver and precious stones remain at the judgment seat of Christ. Three massive reasons you should shake off the chains of childhood and embrace with courage the responsibilities and pressures of adulthood.

Third, we know based upon observation, secular studies, and a mountain of cultural evidence that your culture is adrift and at a loss for where to go and how to get there. Mr. Arnett defines young adulthood as a period of instability, self-focus, and a sustained sense of being in limbo.

Fourth, we know that pop-psychology applauds this lunacy and calls it exploration and self-discovery. In other words, the scientists who study people in their twenties are curious about your behavior and are interested to see where it takes you. Sort of makes you feel like someone's science project, doesn't it?

Fifth, we know that marketing analysts hope to keep you unstable and in limbo for as long as they can. If you stay in limbo, you'll keep buying iPods, snowboards, and cell phones. Forget the fact that you're ruining your life, so long as you can still spend cash!

For what it's worth—you won't read in secular articles or books about any of the rewards we discussed. They *study* you, but they don't have any *answers* for you. They're at a loss too! But God isn't.

On September 3, 1975, Dale Webster surrendered his life. You've probably never heard of him, unless you're a surfer. He surrendered his life to *surfing*. He fully committed himself to the cause of surfing every day for a twenty-eight year lunar cycle—that's 10,407 days in a row. He determined that no job, no relationship, no sickness, and no distance would ever come between him and surfing. In his own words, he was willing to pay a high price, "Sometimes I think of all the things I'll have missed in my life because of this. The only thing I'll have is the memory of riding all those waves...." Webster quit jobs when they threatened his quest. He never journeyed farther than a few hours from the shoreline of his Bodega Bay home in Northern California.

On February 29, 2004, Dale ventured into the water one last time—it was day 10,407 and his life mission was complete. When asked what he would do the next day, Dale responded, "I can't really see not going surfing tomorrow. It's another day, and that's what I do, surf every day."

And for twenty-eight years, the god of surfing took great care of Dale. The only reward he ever achieved was a new wetsuit from O'Neill, and even that was because he was free publicity to the manufacturer.

As he returned to shore on February 29, 2004, he said, "Anybody can do what I did. If you love it enough, you can do anything. All you have to do is start surfing today, and not stop until 2032." Looking into his future, Dale had big plans. At fifty-five years of age, he was looking forward to hitting the road and surfing every surf-spot in the United States.

For twenty-eight years, surfing told Dale what to wear, where to live, where to work, and what to do—if that's not a god, then I don't know what is! Like I said, Dale surrendered his life.

To what purpose will you surrender your life? To what cause will you give your efforts, your days, your time, and your strength? You must make a choice. Indeed, you *will* make a choice—and the passing of years will reveal it.

You are worth more than a surfboard and a spot in the Guinness Book of World Records. You are worth more than a ball, a glove, a net, a skateboard, a computer, a musical instrument or whatever else would attempt to be your god in life. You'll want more at age fifty-five than a good wetsuit rash to show for your life. Dale often referred to his life goal as a quest, and interestingly he said, "It gave me an *identity* and I just kept at it." He gives us a little glimpse into the emptiness of the completed quest when he made this statement, "I want to be remembered not only for the surfing record, but also for some good things I left behind…" Even the great, almighty "surf-god" let Dale down and left him wondering if his life really mattered.

I'm amazed continually at what pagan people will do for their gods and what Christian people won't do for *theirs*. If a man will give twenty-eight years of his life to a *board on water,* might you find even a fraction of that kind of commitment to your *Creator*? If a man will love a *sport* so passionately, might we love our God with even a portion of that kind of passion?

In Joshua chapter 1, Joshua had just assumed the leadership of the children of Israel after the death of Moses. I wrote extensively about it in *Discover Your Destiny*. He was young, fearful, and in way over his head. God repeatedly told him in chapter 1 to be strong and courageous. Five times God and the children of Israel stand behind Joshua and say, "Be courageous." That's a lot for one chapter! He must have needed the repetition!

Well, beginning with chapter 2, Joshua steps up courageously, embraces responsibility that was far bigger than he was, and he followed God in faith. He led the children of Israel across the Jordan River and into a promised land of fights, wars, and bloody battles. Through the struggle, God gave the victory. It's an amazing book of the Bible that chronicles the conquering of the Promised Land and the divine intervention of God.

In chapter 23, Joshua is an old man. He's tanned, but not from surfing. He's wrinkled, but not from saltwater. He's scarred, but not from shark bites. He and Dale Webster would have had absolutely nothing in common. Different gods, different purposes, and different hearts—they just wouldn't have connected.

In this chapter, Joshua is about to die. But before he does, he surveys his life, calls the children of Israel together, and gives them one final challenge—his last words. Any man's last words are important, so let's read them intently and find out how an old man who followed God felt about his life. Here's what he had to say:

> ...I am old and stricken in age: And ye have seen all that the LORD your God hath done unto all these nations because of you; for the LORD your God is he that hath fought for you. ...Be ye therefore very courageous to keep and to do all that is written in the book of the law of Moses, that ye turn not aside therefrom to the right hand or to the left; That ye come not among these nations, these that remain among you; neither make mention of the name of their gods, nor cause to swear by them, neither serve them, nor bow yourselves unto them: But cleave unto the LORD your God, as ye have done unto this day. For the LORD hath driven out from before you great nations and strong: but as for you, no man hath been able to stand before you unto this day. One man of you shall chase a thousand: for the LORD your God, he it is that fighteth for you, as he hath promised you. Take good heed therefore unto yourselves, that ye love the LORD your God.
> —JOSHUA 23:2–3, 6–11

Now it's *Joshua* saying, "Be courageous! God has brought you this far. God has fought for you and will continue to fight for you. Be courageous to keep God's laws, to reject the gods of the surrounding cultures, and cleave to your true God."

His final admonition, "...love the LORD your God."

Joshua not only got the courage thing, but he looked back on his life with delight! He had fallen in love with his great God and was now passionately pleading with the next generation to do the same.

Dale Webster will never have those twenty-eight years to relive. He gave them to surfing. He surrendered. He presented his body a living sacrifice to waves.

Dale Webster gave his life to surfing and changed "the world surfing record." Joshua gave his life to God and changed world history. Just as the value of any gift is in the giver, so the value of any *life* is in the *god*. You must give your life to *some* god—the god of self, the god of surfing, or the God of salvation!

God's invitation to you, "I beseech you therefore, brethren, by the mercies of God, that ye present your bodies a living sacrifice, holy, acceptable unto God, which is your reasonable service" (Romans 12:1).

We've come a long way in this book. By now, I hope you're fed up with folly and pumped up about the rewards that await you. I hope you're jumping out of your skin with eagerness to embrace God's future for your life. More than anything, I hope you have fallen in love with the God who created you and who values you so highly. Your life will be worth so much more and your future so much brighter if you will wrap your whole self into the significance and value that you have in His heart and His plan.

In the coming chapters I want to help you "get from here to there." I want to explore the passions you must have so that you will one day be like Joshua. I want to help you avoid being an old "surfer dude" and help you become everything that God created you to be.

Part three is the last wave of this study. I would say "hang ten" but there's only five more chapters—see you in the next one!

> *But take diligent heed to do the*
> *commandment and the law...to love the*
> *LORD your God, and to walk in all his*
> *ways, and to keep his commandments, and*
> *to cleave unto him, and to serve him with*
> *all your heart and with all your soul.*
> —JOSHUA 22:5

# PART THREE

# GETTING FROM HERE TO THERE

*Three Godly Passions
of Successful Adulthood*

# GETTING FROM HERE TO THERE

*The awesome rewards of adulthood are most enjoyed by those who embrace biblical principles. It's possible to live a life far beneath the original intent of God. Most people do! They end up spiritually scavenging their way through life rather than enjoying abundant blessings. Do you want an average life or do you want the best life? Do you want a C-minus life or an A-plus life?*

*If you want the best life, then you're going to have to be passionate about some things. You'll need to passionately embrace the biblical principles that will ensure a safe journey into those rewards. In the coming chapters, we will explore three godly passions that will compel you forward. Like wind under the wings of an eagle, these passions must set your course and thrust you into your future with God.*

*Once again, ask God to enlighten the eyes of your understanding as we embrace these godly passions for His glory!*

## CHAPTER NINE

# A PASSION FOR GOD—PART ONE

*Embracing Personal Intimacy with God*

Whenyou were five, where did you run for help if you skinned your knee or scraped an elbow? Probably to Mom or Dad. You immediately looked for someone who cared—someone who loved you—someone you were close to. Right? Part of the emotional struggle of growing up is knowing where to run for help—knowing where to turn for *strength*. You can't always run to Mom and Dad. Many young adults turn to friends, drugs, alcohol, parties, sex, or other pleasures. Some just go to Starbucks and ignore the rest of life. Everyone turns somewhere! Where do you turn? To whom do you run? If you know God personally and if you establish your life upon Him, you don't run at all—you *refuge*. We'll come back to that word, so hang on to it.

In some sense, becoming an adult is about letting go of parental comfort and embracing heavenly comfort. It's about letting go of parental provision only to embrace heavenly provision. If you fail to make the transition—if you don't develop a personal, intimate, passionate relationship with God, life becomes more confusing with every passing year.

## The Most Difficult Year of Life

"You're halfway through the most difficult year of your life." These words were spoken to me, midway through my freshman year of Bible college by a man in his seventies. Coming from a seventy-year-old man, that was a strong statement, and it really put my first year away from home into perspective. He was right. I've had tough times and trials since then, but nothing so relentlessly lonely, agonizingly emotional, and thoroughly transitional as that year. I entered that transition as an eighteen-year-old kid with a close family, a happy childhood, and a lot of dreams and desires, and a few months into it, I found myself spiritually, emotionally, and mentally dazed—as though reality had hit me in the face with a railroad tie!

I was surrounded with friends, classes, and an active college life, but the noise of my internal growing pains drowned out the rest of my life. My heart felt as though it was being crammed through a strainer. Far from home, on my own, and utterly lonely, I found out how unprepared I was for this transition. Emotions called me backward—back home, back to family, back to familiarity, back to comfort. God called me forward—forward in faith, forward in growth, and forward through transition. But it was tough.

My friends were experiencing it too, but for some reason we never talked about it. Strangely, I was immersed in a sea of people facing similar trials but felt utterly alone.

Peace momentarily returned to my heart when I went home for three days at Thanksgiving. Stepping off the plane and into our family minivan released a massive surge of emotions that swept through me like a long awaited sigh of soul. But, all too quickly, Thanksgiving came and went, as did Christmas.

When cold January returned, so did the coldness of life. Like a bitter frostbite on my heart, emotional and spiritual loneliness returned. The ebb and flow of college life kept my mind occupied most of the time. Classes, exams, activities, and projects kept me in motion. But when life slowed down—when those quiet moments came late in the evening—the icy winds haunted my heart. Part of me didn't want this land called adulthood. It wasn't kind. It wasn't warm and welcoming like childhood had been. Something was desperately missing.

I was grateful for good friends, but this was an internal struggle that no surface relationship could fix. There was only one relationship that sustained me through that year— my relationship with God. And so it will be with you. The first and foremost passion of your life, if you courageously embrace God's plan for your life, must be your own *private, personal* relationship with God. God leads us into these kinds of storms to show us His presence in our lives—but we must invite Him in—we must draw near to Him.

In the coming pages, I'm probably not going to be funny. It's hard to be humorous about a subject so vital to your life's quest. This is probably the most important part of this book. The wonderful God that we've studied in recent pages desires to know you and for you to know Him personally. To experience life's best rewards, you must learn how to grow close to Him. Many Christian young adults have some terrible misunderstandings about their relationship with God. Let's pull back the curtain of Scripture and see the truth.

## A Personal "God Moment"

Many "God-moments" remain etched into my memory from my young adult life—moments when God undeniably proved Himself real and present in my life. These moments are what prove God's love and power to you personally, and you *must* have them. You must learn to allow God to show Himself in your life.

One winter afternoon when my spiritual battle was especially intense, I made my way back to my empty dorm room, turned the lights off, fell to my knees, and cried out to God. Part of me wanted to run. Part of me wanted to die. Part of me knew I must grow forward and that only God could give me what I needed. All I said was, "God, I really need you...." I said it out loud, and then I began to weep. That's all I could get out.

I'm not the spooky, "I saw Jesus at the end of my bed" type of person. There was no light, no smoke, no loud voice, no lightning strikes in that moment. But there was God. There was, immediately, the undeniable touch and presence of God in my heart. He heard my cry and responded beyond any shadow of a doubt.

It was as though Jesus entered that room, knelt down beside me, wrapped His arms around my shoulders, and said, "I'm right here, son, and everything's going to be okay."

I knelt there for about an hour and didn't say another word, but God said a lot to me. He ministered to my heart.

> *Adulthood brings burdens of the heart that only Christ can comfort.*

He filled my loneliness, renewed my spirit, strengthened my heart, changed my perspective, and comforted my soul. There in the dark, alone with God, everything became clearer. The fog lifted, the icy wind settled, and it was as if someone opened the door of my heart, lit a Christmas Eve fire, made some hot chocolate, and wrapped my heart up in warmth for an hour.

I could share many such moments with you, both before and after that time. Each one was unique. Each one was unforgettable. Each one was born out of soul restlessness and consternation of heart. Each one led to renewed strength, clear vision, and an unforgettable personal encounter with my great Heavenly Father.

That's what Jesus told us to call Him—Abba—which is the Hebrew word for "dad." In that one word—Abba—we see the huge heart of God revealed toward us in true compassion and fatherly love. He invites you into this kind of relationship. Few people understand that, and few Christians deeply experience it. Yet, He still invites you.

Jesus said, "Behold, I stand at the door, and knock: if any man hear my voice, and open the door, I will come in to him, and will sup with him, and he with me" (Revelation 3:20). In this verse, He is speaking to saved people—those who had already trusted Him. Though they knew Him, apparently He had been shut out of their lives. So, He is knocking—desiring to be let in. He uses a word picture—"and [I] will sup with him, and he with me." The word *sup* means "to have dinner together."

When Dana and I have dinner together, it's an event—intimate, close, warm, loving. There are few things that can touch it in "specialness." We enjoy looking into each other's eyes; we say comforting and encouraging things to each other; we watch the candlelight flicker, and we fall in love all over again.

This is what Jesus desires to do in your heart. He wants to sup with you, for you to know Him and be with Him. This is what happened to me that day when I knelt down and cried out to Him. I opened the door on which He was knocking, and He came in to me and supped with me.

The scary thing is, it's possible to be a Christian and never experience this personal intimacy with Christ. He will not force you. If you don't open the door, He just waits—knocking. He won't kick the door in. If the noise of your life and the rush of your moments don't allow you to pause long enough to open the door and "sup" with Christ, your heart will suffer, indefinitely, deeply hungry.

Tears are a language of the heart that Christ speaks. Loneliness is a yearning of the heart that Christ fills. Growing up is a transition of the heart that Christ navigates. Adulthood brings burdens of the heart that only Christ can comfort. Unless you open the door and "sup," you can only "cope." No one can open the door for you. No one can force you to enter into this intimacy. No other person can duplicate this experience or be this Abba to your soul.

Probably a hundred times, some young adult that I care about deeply, has sat across from my desk, stared blankly for a moment, searched for words, only to come up with tears. On a few occasions, I've talked about this subject in a group setting of "twenty-somethings," and it's like peeling back the layers of surface-ness to reveal the same unrest in every heart in the room. Eyes well up with tears; spiritual hunger surfaces, and reality's railroad tie is back to smack someone else in the face.

I address this soul-emptiness because I remember it all too well. Except now, I can clearly see how pivotal it was to experiencing the rewards we learned about. My heart goes out to you because I remember the distress. My pen goes out to you because I know the answer—Abba.

Can Abba sup with you for a moment? Can the two of you visit personally? Find a quiet place. Get a cup of coffee or hot chocolate. Light a fire. Do something to seclude your heart to what we're about to study. Ask the Lord to venture into these truths with you. Still your heart and the surrounding world and listen to Him. Don't just read *about* an intimate relationship with God—*experience* it right now. Open the door to Abba and let Him come in to you and sup. Let these Scriptures and these principles be time with Him, and let them soothe your heart and heal your wounds. Let's explore eight characteristics that will help you grow close to God and experience true intimacy with Him.

# 1.  A Close Relationship Begins by Birth

Your walk with God is not a *system* you sign up for, but rather a *relationship* you are born into. The writer of Hebrews spent thirteen chapters explaining that Christ offers us a *relationship*, not a *system*, and he capped it off with these verses, "Now the God of peace, that brought again from the dead our Lord Jesus, that great shepherd of the sheep, through the blood of the everlasting covenant, Make you perfect in every good work to do his will, working in you that which is wellpleasing in his sight, through Jesus Christ; to whom be glory for ever and ever. Amen" (Hebrews 13:20-21).

The God of Heaven, our Abba Father, is a God of *covenant*—He binds Himself to His Word. And He desires to enter into a covenant relationship with you—one that is bound by His promise. Like a marriage, He desires to fully give Himself to you forever and to accept you completely as you are. His covenant is explained in Hebrews 8:12, "For I will be merciful to their unrighteousness, and their sins and their iniquities will I remember no more." He offers the full pardon and forgiveness of your sins through the sacrifice of Jesus on the Cross. He says in Hebrews 9:27-28, "And as it is appointed unto men once to die, but after this the judgment: So Christ was once offered to bear the sins of many; and unto them that look for him shall he appear the second time without sin unto salvation." Christ paid for your sins on the Cross, and He offers you total salvation—the opportunity to be "born" into His family spiritually and to become His child. This way, when you face death, you will be certain that you have eternal life and salvation.

Jesus called this salvation a "second birth" in John 3:3, "...Verily, verily, I say unto thee, Except a man be born again, he cannot see the kingdom of God." Later in that passage, Jesus continues, "For God so loved the world, that he gave his only begotten Son, that whosoever believeth in him should not perish, but have everlasting life."

You cannot know God and draw close to Him until you are *born* into His family. Spiritual birth happens when you realize you are separated from God by sin and that Jesus, God in the flesh, personally paid the penalty for your sin. "Spiritual repentance" means that you recognize your condition in sin and your need for a Saviour and turn to Christ with a *full heart belief* in Him as your only Saviour. In that moment, you are born into God's family—you become His child, and He becomes your Abba.

Having Christ as your personal Saviour means you have a guaranteed Heavenly Father in this life, and a guaranteed place in Heaven after you die. Jesus said, "…I am the way, the truth, and the life: no man cometh unto the Father, but by me" (John 14:6). In other words, you can't get to Heaven any other way except through Christ.

Has this happened in your life? Do you remember your spiritual birth? If you cannot recall the moment that you placed your one hundred percent belief in Jesus Christ as your only Saviour, then I urge you to make that decision right now. This is where intimacy with God begins. I encourage you to pray a simple prayer of faith—something like this: "Dear Jesus, I believe that you are God, that you died on the cross for my sins, and that you rose again from the dead. I confess that I am a sinner. I ask you to come into my heart, to be my personal Saviour, and to give me your gift of eternal life."

This is a decision of faith that simply claims God's promise—His covenant. If you struggle with faith, then you'd better not spend too much time thinking about life, because everything in life is a faith proposition—from driving down the street, to flying on an airplane, to eating restaurant food, to riding a theme park ride. In every case, you're blindly trusting people you don't know to do the right thing—and in every case, your life depends on it! If you'll place your life in the hands of oncoming drivers whom you've never met, might it be safer to place your life into the hands of a faithful Heavenly Father?

Placing faith in God is far more reasonable than placing faith in strangers who built an aircraft, prepared your dinner, or maintained a roller coaster! Choosing Christ for salvation requires less faith than any of those things, and there's absolutely no risk—nothing to lose. He will never let you down. He will keep His covenant.

The rest of life is *risky* faith—faith in God is strictly *rewarded* faith, no risk whatsoever! Hebrews 11:6 tells us, "But without faith it is impossible to please him: for he that cometh to God must believe that he is, and that he is a rewarder of them that diligently seek him."

If you have never trusted Christ as your personal Saviour, then I urge you to pause right now in reading this book and make this simple but vital decision. If you are unsure and would like to know more about why this is so important, I encourage you to visit *strivingtogether.com* and download a little book I wrote called *Done*. It's a complimentary download, and it will answer a lot of your questions about how to be born into God's family.

## 2.  A Close Relationship Is Structured but Not Systematic

This is where many young adults get off course in their relationship with God. We tend to gravitate to "systematic" because it feels achievable—like something we can check off our "to-do" lists. Making God a "to-do" on your list will make you temporarily feel *spiritual*, but it will also make you feel *distant* from Him. Relating with God is not so different from relating to anyone else you love—except you can't see Him visibly or hear Him audibly.

God doesn't want your systematic love—He doesn't want forced, unnatural, required love. He told His people repeatedly to put away their *systems* when their *hearts* were far from Him. He wants your *heart*. He desires voluntary, sincere, pure love from a willing heart.

At the same time, while this relationship isn't systematic, it will have *structure*. Any healthy relationship has guidelines—things you will and won't do because of love for the other. The Bible is filled with instruction—structure that teaches us what pleases and displeases God.

Think of it this way. Let's say you have a close friend, and you are concerned about developing a healthy relationship and growing close. If you focus on a system of developing that relationship, it will quickly become forced and heartless. Relationships are not machines. But, you *will* have structure in growing that relationship. You will have guidelines that you would follow in relating to that friend. For instance, you probably wouldn't spit on her, slap him in the face, or call her names. This isn't legalism; it's just reasonable structure that gives your relationship some sensible boundaries.

In another example, growing close to my wife requires structure—I will be faithful to her; I will not kiss another woman. I will help around the house. I will not burp in public. I will tell her what time to expect me home, etc. Yet, the relationship is not about structure—it's about our love for each other. The structure just provides the framework on which the rest of the relationship can grow. You might say it's the skeleton of the relationship—the structure that holds it together.

The moment you begin to spend time with God out of obligation is the moment God distances Himself. James 4:8 says, "Draw nigh to God, and he will draw nigh to you." Rigid, systematic, routine love repels God, but sincere love draws Him closer. Obligated love doesn't delight Him. Whatever is systematic about your relationship is probably the very thing that is killing your heart for God. Everything you do for God must flow from a pure heart of love or it means nothing.

Focusing on the structure or reducing your walk with God to a system is the quickest way to kill closeness with

Him. Eventually your whole Christian life loses heart and becomes mundane and frustrating. This kind of systematic, lukewarm, heartless approach to God literally makes Him sick. "So then because thou art lukewarm, and neither cold nor hot, I will spue thee out of my mouth" (Revelation 3:16).

There is a popular teaching about grace that says God isn't interested in *how* you live; He just looks at your heart. This is as ridiculous as saying that my wife doesn't care how I live as long as I really, really love her. God cares intimately about your lifestyle. He desires you to be like Christ—pure and holy. But He also cares that it be sincere and motivated by His grace in your heart. This verse explains both sides of the equation, "Let us draw near with a true heart in full assurance of faith, having our hearts sprinkled from an evil conscience, and our bodies washed with pure water" (Hebrews 10:22). "Draw near with a true heart"—make sure your love is sincere and not systematic. "Having our hearts sprinkled from an evil conscience"—come to Him with a clean life and a pure conscience.

When you are drawing close to God, think *pure relationship*, not *starchy system*. Gravitate away from system. You cannot box God into ten minutes in the morning or five minutes in the evening.

Along these lines, be careful that you don't define "church" as something from which you gravitate away! Your weekly church attendance is critical to your personal relationship with Christ. If Jesus found it necessary to worship God and hear the teaching of His Word in a corporate setting, you should too. If Jesus loved the church enough to die for it, you should love it enough to make it a priority in your life. Faithfulness to a Bible-believing church should be a part of the *structure* that supports your heart for God.

In pleasing God, your life *will* have *structure*—you will follow God's guidelines for right living and a holy lifestyle. But don't allow your relationship to become *systematic*. He's not a "to-do"—He's not a religious system—He's a God who desires intimate, personal, true-heart love.

## 3. A Close Relationship Is Developed through Time

Drawing close to God requires private time alone with Him. It requires that you quiet your world and enter His presence. It requires that you still the whirlwind of activity and that you draw near with a pure heart to listen to His still small voice. He invites you to "come boldly unto the throne of grace, that we may obtain mercy, and find grace to help in time of need" (Hebrews 4:16). We've already seen that He *knocks*. We've seen that word *sup*, which implies a season of time spent together. The more you do this, the more you will know Him and the closer you will become to Him. Let's look more closely at what this time involves and how it works.

*Time with God requires communication.* Just as time spent with a friend involves conversation and sharing your heart, even so, your time with God should involve communication to and from Him. Communication *from* Him is His written Word. Embrace it, read it daily, meditate on it daily, and let it saturate your heart constantly. God's Word is His love letter of life instruction to you. It will comfort, convict, strengthen, and settle you. It will speak to you no matter where you are in life or what circumstances you are facing. You must make His Word a daily priority in your life.

Communication *to* Him involves prayer. It involves crying out to Him, bearing your heart, and sharing your requests. It involves telling Him your love and adoration and thanking Him for His goodness and power. He invites you into this relationship every day, and you must enter into it if you are to survive the journey.

***Time with God requires consistency.*** While this relationship shouldn't be *systematic*, it should be *consistent*. If I neglect my wife or kids for extended periods of time, we grow apart. If you neglect any close friend for a season, relational distance is inevitable! It's quite simple really. To stay close, we must spend time together consistently—we must rank high on each other's calendars. Inconsistent time weakens relationships, and it does the same between you and God. Honestly, I don't think it matters much to God if you spend twenty minutes a day with Him or two hours every other day—so long as you are consistent in spending time alone with Him. The goal would be to spend time with Him every day, but don't get so systematic that you lose the dynamic of relationship!

I know young adults that really beat themselves up if they missed a day in their devotions or if they fell asleep the last time they prayed. Don't you think God knows you were tired? He understands the chaos of your life better than anyone else. My kids don't beat me up if I go a day without seeing them; why would God? At the same time, I don't want to neglect Him! I'm not saying intentionally skip your devotions; I'm just saying it's not a system. Missing yesterday doesn't mean you're a *failure*, and having them doesn't necessarily mean you're a *success*! It's all about your heart! Be consistent, but don't obsess over a system—make it real and personal.

***Time with God must have quantity.*** I have noticed something in ministry and family. I can't build a good relationship in a hurry. Relationships can't be rushed like FedEx packages. There's no "overnight" option. People I love don't want five minutes a month—they need a lunch hour, a conversation, and some quantity time.

Healthy families spend large amounts of time together. And healthy Christians spend large amounts of time with God. More than five rushed minutes a day, you need several hours (or more) a week when you can be alone in God's presence. Your relationship cannot be *rushed* and still be *meaningful*. This is what Jesus means when He says, "Abide in me, and I in you. As the branch cannot bear fruit of itself, except it abide in the vine; no more can ye, except ye abide in me" (John 15:4).

There are countless ways to spend quantity time with God. Take a long walk or bike ride with Him and talk out loud to Him. Find a park where you can read a scriptural book or spend an hour listening to godly music. Speak with Him while you're driving or jogging. Invite Him into the mundane and routine things of life. He cares about every detail of your life and desires to be a part of every moment.

***Time with God must have continuity.*** Healthy time with God must be *uninterrupted*. It must be focused upon Christ and exclusively His. I've noticed that my communication with anyone is hindered when Fox News is on! I'm a one-track minded person. When my mind is on one thing, it could take as long as three minutes to change channels mentally. Even so, God wants your *focus*—and you already have His. It's not like He's distracted by running the universe and doesn't have time for you. Why would you offer Him less? He wants your focused heart. "A double minded man is unstable in all his ways" (James 1:8).

> *Recognize His presence and practice His presence all day long.*

Think of these points this way. Your private time with God should be *unrushed, unstructured,* and *uninterrupted.* As in any relationship, you'll have days when this kind of time is *less* and days when it is *more*—but it ought to get first priority, and it must remain highly relational rather than systematic.

Listen to the invitation of God, "And ye shall seek me, and find me, when ye shall search for me with all your heart" (Jeremiah 29:13). Seeking and searching require time and focus—whether you're searching for your lost car keys, your missing brain, or your lost closeness with God.

Another word that bears out this thought of spending time with God is *refuge*. Psalm 91:2 says, "I will say of the LORD, He is my refuge and my fortress: my God; in him will I trust." Repeatedly God refers to Himself as a refuge—which is literally a shelter or a place to dwell. He also calls Himself a dwelling place, "LORD, thou hast been our dwelling place in all generations" (Psalm 90:1).

Do you get it? God *desires* time with you. You desperately *need* time with Him. He's not in a hurry. You have His undivided attention. You determine the schedule and the agenda—He's just waiting to sup. He is everything you need, and He will meet you anytime, anywhere. He invites you to find refuge in Him, abide in Him, and dwell in Him. Settle down and stay a while. There's no better *time* in all the world! Your heart will never be the same after you spend time with God!

On another level entirely, your relationship with God should never really pause. It should be continual throughout every moment of every day. He invites us in 1 Thessalonians 5:17 to "Pray without ceasing." He desires to be your companion through every thought, every moment, and every circumstance. He desires to be in all of your thoughts. "The wicked, through the pride of his countenance, will not seek after God: God is not in all his thoughts" (Psalm 10:4). Recognize His presence and practice His presence all day long—that way every activity of life becomes a part of your growing relationship with your Creator.

Throughout your life, you will be overwhelmed by circumstances beyond your control and things you just don't understand. These things will either cause you to stand frozen in time, or cause you to flee to God. Isaiah 40:29-31 says, "He giveth power to the faint; and to them that have no might he increaseth strength. Even the youths shall faint and be weary, and the young men shall utterly fall: But they that wait upon the LORD shall renew their strength; they shall mount up with wings as eagles; they shall run, and not be weary; and they shall walk, and not faint."

In other words, you *will* grow weary and faint. It is inevitable. You will enter seasons of life that you don't understand. You will face times of spiritual battle and emotional struggle that are bigger than you are. Where will you turn? Will you run? Will you hide? Or will you *refuge* to God?

God's promise in this verse is that if you will "wait" upon Him, He will renew your strength. That word *wait* literally means "to bind up together as if by twisting." It's far more than passive patience. It is active. It involves drawing close, binding, and twisting your life into God—finding and establishing your identity in Him. It's spending time privately, personally with Him. And as you do, He will renew your strength and thrust you forward on eagle's wings!

To this point, we've seen that personal intimacy with God involves being *born* into His family, is *structured* but not *systematic*, and is developed through *time*—unrushed, unstructured, and uninterrupted. In the next chapter we'll look at five more essential qualities of this incredible relationship.

See you there.

## CHAPTER TEN

# A PASSION FOR GOD—PART TWO

*Embracing Personal Intimacy with God*

It's time for a word puzzle. Can you find the one consistency in all of these verses?

And the LORD was with Joseph, and he was a prosperous man....—GENESIS 39:2

And his master saw that the LORD was with him, and that the LORD made all that he did to prosper in his hand.—GENESIS 39:3

So the LORD was with Joshua; and his fame was noised throughout all the country.—JOSHUA 6:27

And Samuel grew, and the LORD was with him, and did let none of his words fall to the ground.—I SAMUEL 3:19

And Saul was afraid of David, because the LORD was with him, and was departed from Saul.—I SAMUEL 18:12

> Behold, a virgin shall be with child, and shall bring forth
> a son, and they shall call his name Emmanuel, which
> being interpreted is, God with us.—MATTHEW 1:23

These passages refer to God being *with* us. Wouldn't you like to go through life knowing that God is *with you*? What an awesome way to live life—God with you, His eye upon you, His hand guiding you! There is no greater relationship in life.

We're studying eight principles of developing intimacy with God. We've seen so far that closeness with God begins at *birth*, develops *relationally* not systematically, and grows through *time*. Let's press forward and discover the last five principles.

## 4.   A Close Relationship Requires Transparency

Transparency is a word that scares a lot of people. In fact, most people go through life with an inner fear of being exposed. They fear the truth being known. They work at building fancy facades and artificial covers in life, and their greatest threat would be for someone to see them as they truly are.

To some extent, this thinking has tainted your life and no doubt your relationship with God. Ever hear someone pray one of those impressive, flowery prayers? Ever pray to God but not really mean what you're saying? Ever read your Bible or spend time with God when your heart is a million miles away or your thoughts have drifted off to that last love note you received?

Let me remind you—God knows all your secrets, and He's still in love with you. God is intimately acquainted with all of your failures, yet still He desires to be with you. God sees straight through you. He knows when you're too tired to pray, too weary to want Him, and too distracted by carnality to be real. He sees it all and knows it all. Yet, He still loves you and patiently works within you.

This is where *transparency* comes in. You can't be *close* to God until you can be *real* with Him. You can't fool Him. He doesn't buy your act. In fact, it repels Him. Hypocrisy is like a stiff-arm to God—it keeps Him distant. Transparency with God is merely admitting to Him what He already knows about you. Transparency is facing who you really are with God. It's the first step to transformation and closeness. He can't change you if you aren't real. He can't be close to you if you are faking it.

Scripture reveals that men who were close to God were *real* with Him. Moses doubted and told God. So did Thomas. Peter put his foot in his mouth more than a few times. Even John the Baptist sent messengers to Jesus asking if He was really the Messiah—after he had spent his whole life preaching about Him. Think about that! John the Baptist *heard* God's voice from Heaven when he baptized Jesus. Yet, months later John's doubts surfaced, and he became transparent with God.

God doesn't squash questions or kill transparent people. He doesn't strike doubts with lightning—He answers them and responds to them. He changes the hearts that are *honest* before Him.

You see, when you put up a front with God, it's like closing your heart to Him. You forbid Him access to your heart, and He can't change what He can't access! Sincere transparency places your heart in the molding hands of God where He can transform it and make it more like Christ's.

If you're angry with God, it would be better to tell Him and to seek His grace than it would be to bury it or try to hide it. He already knows. If you are struggling with a bad spirit, it would be better to open up and confess it than to try to fake God out. He already sees. If you don't understand and your doubts are driving you crazy, take them to God. He's not surprised. If you are second guessing His plan, tell Him and ask for clarity. He's well aware of your condition, and your problems can only be solved when you become transparent with God.

Ignoring issues of the heart in God's presence would be like lying to a doctor who is trying to help me. If I have cancer but I'm misleading the doctor about my symptoms, I'm only hurting myself. To get treatment for my cancer, I must be transparent about my symptoms. A doctor can't diagnose what I hide.

As with any relationship, if you can't be real with God, then you can't be close to Him, and He can't change you.

## 5.  A Close Relationship Strengthens through Commitment

Your personal relationship with God will only be as strong as your personal commitment to Him. For some, God is a distant figure; for some He's an occasional "good-luck" charm; and for others, He is everything! To grow close to God, He must be *everything,* and you must fully commit to Him.

In 1 Kings 18:21 we see a mirror image of this generation when it comes to commitment, "And Elijah came unto all the people, and said, How long halt ye between two opinions? if the Lord be God, follow him: but if Baal, then follow him. And the people answered him not a word." They couldn't make up their minds about God! They refused to commit.

The twixter generation is in this exact same spiritual position—and collectively they are *answering not a word.* This generation has lost the ability to commit to a decision, much less to God. The mentality of culture is, "try it and *see* if it will work out for *me.*" We want to explore our options rather than commit to our God.

Can I burst this bubble for a moment? When you approach any life commitment with a "try and see" mentality, forget it—it won't work. Any marriage that starts with this thinking is failed before it starts. Any life calling that begins with this thinking is over before it begins. I'm sorry, but as long as you have a flip-flop mentality on core values and core commitments, your life just won't work out!

Joshua knew this, so he challenged the people, "And if it seem evil unto you to serve the LORD, choose you this day whom ye will serve; whether the gods which your fathers served that were on the other side of the flood, or the gods of the Amorites, in whose land ye dwell: but as for me and my house, we will serve the LORD" (Joshua 24:15). He called the people to commit—to make their choice final forever!

In just sixty-five short years America has gone from "the greatest generation" to "the faintest generation"! Sixty-five years ago our grandparents and great-grandparents were dropping their plans, sacrificing their dreams, and going to war. Collectively, they put the future on hold to *save* the future. Young ladies went to work in factories building ships, making bullets, and packing bombs. Young men trained quickly and went to war. Hundreds of thousands of them gave their lives to conquer two of history's worst dictators at the same time. Failure was not an option. Victory was the only acceptable outcome, and they won. They committed fully and preserved freedom as we know it.

Now sixty-five years later, our generation is fumbling. We're just not sure about anything! Commitment scares us to death. We want all the benefits of commitment without the risk or the burden. But it doesn't work that way. If you want the rewards we talked about, you must learn to commit—to God and to His principles.

You need the ability to make a decision that will never be reconsidered. When I surrendered to serve God with my life, that decision was not up for reconsideration, and it never has been. It was graven in the foundation of my heart and is not up for discussion. Somewhere between my youth and yours, we've lost that ability. In today's culture, every decision and every value is up for recall! A decision made today may mean nothing tomorrow. A calling today may be relegated to emotionalism a year from now. A passionate resolve today might be just a passing fad tomorrow. This is sad.

You must reclaim the lost art of commitment! It is critical to your future. What does it matter if you believe in God if you cannot fully trust Him? What does it matter if you love God if you cannot wholly commit to Him?

I challenge you to reject the "try it and see" mentality of your culture. Your relationship with God will never grow with that mindset. Forget a solid marriage, forget a life's calling, forget having a life of eternal significance if you can't commit.

I challenge you right now to fully commit your life to your great God. You've seen how much He loves you and how awesome His plans are for you. Engrave your heart with a commitment to Him that can never be overturned or reconsidered. Allow Him to build into you a firm resolve that will commit and never question. Commit to His truth, His will, and His core values for your life. Establish some non-negotiable values—things that will never be up for discussion.

Every good decision is tested, and beyond the testing is the fruit of the decision. Don't be surprised when your resolve is tested. Don't be shocked when a good decision leads you into a trying time! And don't start second-guessing! Don't uproot a commitment you made just because it got hard to keep. God rewards commitment, and getting through the tough stuff is the only path to the rewards.

Learn to dig in your heels and refuse to reconsider the things that you know to be true and right. Grow some roots in God and don't let every breeze threaten to knock you over. Psalm 1 tells us that God wants you to become like a tree firmly rooted and abundantly fruitful, but for that to happen, you must fully commit to His path.

Your *relationship* with God will only be as strong as your *commitment* to Him. He's not a good-luck charm. He's the

Sovereign God of the universe, and He deserves the throne of your heart for the rest of your life.

## 6.  A Close Relationship Solidifies through Trust

This is another glaring problem in relating to God. He scares us. His plans worry us. We wonder what He has in mind. We are nervous about what He's up to. We view Him as a threat to our plans rather than the fulfiller of our dreams. We simply don't trust Him. We eye Him with suspicion like a shady character at a bank ATM. We suspect that He's going to invade our lives and rob our dreams.

How can you grow close to a person you don't trust? Our distrust of God keeps us distant from Him. It's like a ten-foot pole that keeps us apart. We're saying, "God, I love you, I want to go to Heaven, but I just don't want you to mess with my life!"

I feel sorry for young adults with this heart. They're missing the rewards! Proverbs 3:5–6 says, "Trust in the LORD with all thine heart; and lean not unto thine own understanding. In all thy ways acknowledge him, and he shall direct thy paths." Psalm 37:3 says, "Trust in the LORD, and do good; so shalt thou dwell in the land, and verily thou shalt be fed." Psalm 115:11 says, "Ye that fear the LORD, trust in the LORD: he is their help and their shield." And finally, Psalm 118:8 says, "It is better to trust in the LORD than to put confidence in man."

Throughout all of Scripture God is saying to mankind—*trust me*! He can be trusted! You can fully trust Him with your whole future, and He will never fail you. He will constantly delight you.

Having your trust *matters* to God! It is why you were created. There's a word in Scripture that relates to our trust in God. It's the word *marvel*. Stay with me.

*Marvel* literally means "to admire with wonder." When you see it in Scripture, it usually refers to people marveling at Christ. They marveled at His miracles, His words, His healing. He is a pretty amazing God! When men saw Jesus they dropped their jaws and stood in stunned, surprised wonderment—they marveled.

But there are two times in Scripture when *Jesus* marvels. What does it take to make God stand back in surprised wonder and admiration? What does it take to make God's jaw drop and His eyes widen? Well, in Matthew 8:10 Jesus marveled at the *belief* of the Roman centurion. *Trust* made His jaw drop with amazement!

The second time, in Mark 6:6 Jesus marveled, but this time it was a different story. He was in His hometown, trying to teach, trying to heal, trying to do miracles, but He couldn't. The Bible says, "And he could there do no mighty work, save that he laid his hands upon a few sick folk, and healed them. And he marvelled because of their unbelief" (Mark 6:5–6). His hands were tied! The God of the universe was strapped down and "could there do no mighty work." Why? *Distrust*. They didn't believe.

So outrageously ridiculous was their unbelief that once again, Jesus stood back, dropped His jaw, and marveled. He wondered at the fact that they wouldn't trust Him.

When you trust God, you untie His hands to do mighty works in your life. When you fail to trust Him, you prevent Him. Trust is what unlocks God's power and presence in your life. Trust is what God desires most from you. Hebrews 11:6, "But without faith it is impossible to please him...." Trust is sticking your neck out with God—taking a risk that isn't really a risk at all!

Finally, trust starts small and grows over time. God isn't intimidated by small faith. He only asks for a little trust, and He's willing to build from there. You must begin somewhere, and God says, "start small." In Luke 17:6 we see, "And the Lord said, If ye had faith as a grain of mustard seed, ye might say unto this sycamine tree, Be thou plucked up by the root, and be thou planted in the sea; and it should obey you." "A grain of mustard seed"—start small and let's build on that! God will prove Himself faithful and trustworthy in the smallest of details. He's willing to grow your faith over time. He's willing to prove Himself and earn your trust—but you must give Him something to work with. Start with a mustard-seed trust and let God prove Himself. He will.

## 7.    A Close Relationship Becomes Intimate through Exclusivity

God isn't interested in sharing the spotlight. A close relationship with Him requires *exclusivity*—He must be your only God. He commands this in Exodus 20:3, "Thou shalt have no other gods before me." He warns us in Matthew 6:24 that "no man can serve two masters...." But why?

Intimacy is only possible through *exclusivity*. For instance, when I asked Dana to marry me, I was looking for an intimate setting. I didn't reserve a table for fifteen, I reserved a table for two. Intimacy requires exclusivity.

This is why culture is so off-base in the area of moral purity. Physical relations between a man and a woman were designed by God to produce spiritual and relational intimacy between two people committed to each other for life. Period. It's not merely an act of pleasure. It's not meant to be shared outside of marriage. And the cultural philosophy of "sex with anybody, anywhere, anytime" is destroying any possibility of true intimacy. Intimacy in your future marriage will be possible to the degree that you are exclusively each other's! Having a history of sex partners not only messes up your life in the near-term, it makes future intimacy very difficult and permanently flawed.

As a side note, I'm not condemning you if you have failed in this area, but I challenge you to claim God's grace, make your heart right before Him, and commit anew to living by His principles regarding sexual purity. God will give you a second chance, and His grace will restore you in ways that nothing else can!

The *only* recipe for the most intimate and joyful marriage is moral purity before marriage and then total exclusivity inside of marriage bound by irreversible commitment! Did you get that? Read it again—it's important!

Even so, the only recipe for intimacy with God is heart purity before Him, total exclusivity with Him bound by irreversible commitment to Him. He must be your only God. If you try to share the throne of your heart among lesser gods, you will end up distant from the true God.

King David was a "man after God's own heart." There was never a question of who David's God was. He was exclusive in his relationship with God. He made some mistakes and bad decisions, but he never had other gods. He was God's alone.

His son, Solomon started out that way. In fact, he was so committed that God offered him whatever he wanted. When Solomon asked for wisdom, God was so pleased that He promised Solomon both wisdom and riches. What a great God!

But somewhere along the way Solomon made a very foolish choice. We saw it earlier. Ecclesiastes 1:17, "And I gave my heart to know wisdom, and to know madness and folly: I perceived that this also is vexation of spirit." Solomon gave his heart to know folly—particularly sexual folly. He had three hundred wives and seven hundred concubines. In Solomon's day, a concubine was sort of a secondary or inferior wife. Essentially, Solomon had one thousand wives. (One thousand mothers-in-law? Maybe he wasn't so wise after all.) In so doing, he blatantly disobeyed several of God's commands. Among those commands was one that forbade him to marry into pagan culture. God warned him that a pagan wife would turn his heart away to false gods.

This is exactly what happened. A few years after taking pagan wives, Solomon was trying to mix his God with false gods. He was placating to his pagan wives and giving in to their nagging. He didn't reject God, but he did try to push Him aside for other gods.

Just one generation later, Solomon's son was not only rejecting God, but he was allowing pagan worship of the most vulgar sorts. The children of Israel were taking their newborn babies, their sons, and their daughters and burning them alive to false gods.

A couple hundred years later, God rehearses His grievances against this nation in 2 Kings 17. It's not a pretty picture. In verse 17, He says, "And they caused their sons and their daughters to pass through the fire, and used divination and enchantments, and sold themselves to do evil in the sight of the LORD, to provoke him to anger." In this passage God was angry with a people who were utterly perverse and degenerate.

*The only recipe for intimacy with God is heart purity before Him.*

Where did it start? What could possibly take an entire nation from being the people of God under King David to being an immoral, godless, pagan people burning their children alive? What could cause such a radical reversal in less than one generation?

Idolatry. Solomon simply tried to share God's space with pagans. He tried to minimize Him. He wasn't quite as "fanatical" as his father. One son later, kids are being sacrificed to the fire of false gods.

Solomon tried to be "seeker-sensitive" rather than God-sensitive. He tried to marginalize God to maximize his own popularity. He tried to mix God with the world, but it didn't work. Over hundreds of years, a nation floundered in wickedness, paganism, idolatry, and captivity as a result of one father who gave his heart to both wisdom and folly at the same time. He basically said, "I want to know God and sin. I want to love God and the world. I want to experience both sides!"

He regretted his decision. He messed up his life, his family, and an entire nation. You too will regret marginalizing God. He's either God exclusively, or not God at all. Make your choice. He will not share His throne.

## 8.   A Close Relationship Thrives on Submission

This is big. Submission scares us almost as much as trust does. This word makes us feel like we're losing control, and we love to feel like we're *in control*! Submitting to another seems like a loss of freedom and independence. Yet, with God, *submitting* is *winning*.

In James 4:7 God commands, "Submit yourselves therefore to God...." The word *submit* means "to reflexively obey." It implies an instant, total trust that immediately complies with willing obedience. It is not forced. It is not obligated. This kind of submission involves glad-hearted surrender to the will of another. God commands that we first submit to *Him*, then He commands that we submit to *one another*. "Submitting yourselves one to another in the fear of God" (Ephesians 5:21).

Would you like to take your intimacy with God to the next level? Would you like to really *know* Him? Then *obey* Him. Find that area where you are resisting Him and give in. What are you doing that you *know* God doesn't approve of? What are you *not* doing that you *know* God wants you to do? Give in.

Recently, a young lady I know was developing a dating relationship with a young man that she *knew* was not God's will for her future. The relationship was emotionally interesting and attractive to her, but at the heart something was wrong. After some searching and praying, this young lady submitted to what she *knew* was God's will. She broke it off. Tough decision? You bet. But something happened that she didn't expect. God's peace returned to her heart. Without even realizing it, she had alienated God, which negatively affected the rest of her life. She was knowingly resisting what she *knew* God wanted, which created spiritual distance and inner turmoil. Submission was the answer. Though it was a tough decision, the peace and closeness with God that returned to her heart was well worth it!

In Ephesians 5:17 God says, "Wherefore be ye not unwise, but understanding what the will of the Lord is." In your heart, you already know what God's will is in many areas of your life. But *understanding* God's will and *submitting* to God's will are two different things. Where are you resisting God in your life right now? Your whole heart and relationship with God will change the moment you give in!

Dana loves the Olive Garden Restaurant. I don't. Submission is choosing to like Olive Garden because my wife does, and then gladly taking her there simply because I love her.

Submission shows the highest level of trust. Submission to God doesn't *contemplate* His commands, *reason through* His expectations, or *second-guess* His goodness. Submission trusts so much and with such abandon that it obeys *now* and thinks *later*. Submission jumps and then asks "how high"—and with a great attitude!

> *Submission to God obeys now and thinks later.*

There's something very important about submission that you need to know. God submitted to *you* before He ever commanded you to submit to *Him*. Philippians 2:8 says of Jesus, "And being found in fashion as a man, he humbled himself, and became obedient unto death, even the death of the cross." Jesus willingly went to death for you. He submitted to your need. He gladly gave everything, to give what you most needed. That is total self-abandonment—submission. So, with God, when you choose to submit to Him, you're only giving *Him* what He already gave *you*!

God *deserves* your all! He created you. He bought you back. He owns you. You are not your own. He could force you to submit, but He refuses to do that. He gives you a free will. Yet, this radical abandonment to God is *reasonable* in light of His radical abandonment to you! It is "your reasonable service" (Romans 12:1).

Here's the best part. When any relationship has mutual submission, there is great intimacy. When any two persons give themselves wholly for the other—each giving the other his best—a strong, close relationship is the product.

In the business world this is called a "win-win" agreement. In God's economy, total submission to Him means you win! Do you get it? Maybe this will help you understand it, "He that findeth his life shall lose it: and he that loseth his life for my sake shall find it" (Matthew 10:39). The gospels record this statement of Jesus six times! He repeatedly tried to tell people, "Give me your whole life and you win!"

Let me illustrate. Pretend that you and I are sitting at a table discussing this principle, and a very wealthy man challenges us to arm-wrestle as many times as we can in ten minutes. He promises that every time one of us wins he will give the winner one million dollars. I don't know about you, but I'd be pretty happy about that offer.

So, we lock wrists, start the clock, and the wrestling begins. If we're stupid, we resist each other. Valuable seconds are ticking away while we're locked upright—wrist against wrist. Let's say that a minute goes by goes by before you finally win. (Of course, I let you.) Congratulations you have a million dollars and nine minutes left. Let's say that another minute goes by before I finally win. Now *I* have a million dollars. Eight minutes left. Bottom line is, we're both *idiots*.

Let's rewind the clock and start over. Only this time, let's come to a *mutual submission* agreement. Let's agree to give in to each other. Let's *let* each other win as many times as we can. So, the clock starts and right away you win, then right away I win, then you again, then me again. Three seconds have gone by and we both already have two million dollars! After ten minutes we'd both be hundreds of millions of dollars richer than if we had spent the same ten minutes *resisting* each other.

Now, this only works when both parties agree to submit to each other. It's called win-win—mutual submission. Resistance kills a relationship, but submission builds it! God already let you win. He died on the Cross and gave you everything. He gave in already. Now it's your turn. Are you going to win and keep winning, or will you lose everything because you refuse to submit? It's your choice.

Submission to God isn't losing—it's *winning*! He already submitted to you, and when you submit to Him, you win too.

## When Relational Distance Leads to Disaster

Brian Wells didn't have much and didn't need much. He lived in a small white cottage in Erie, Pennsylvania, in August of 2003. He lived a contented, frugal lifestyle. He was a 46-year-old pizza deliveryman with a simple life and a happy personality. He delivered pizzas for thirty years.

Just before 2:00 PM August 28, 2003, the phone rang at Mamma Mia Pizzeria and a man placed an order. Moments later, Brian was delivering the order to what ended up being a dead-end dirt road. There he was accosted by a group of men who locked a bomb around his neck and told him to go rob a bank. They warned him not to delay, disobey, or warn anyone or the bomb would detonate.

The men then activated a timer on the device and told him he had a little over an hour to carry out the robbery and three other demands.

Fearing for his life, Brian obeyed. He got into his car, drove to the bank, and robbed it just as they instructed him. He was on his way to his next stop when police surrounded his car, ordered him out, and immediately handcuffed him. It was then that Brian told them of the bomb. Police immediately retreated to a safe distance, leaving Brian handcuffed outside of his car, sitting crossed legged on the pavement. The time was 2:30 PM.

For nearly an hour, Brian sat on the pavement trying to explain his situation to police. He begged for someone to remove the bomb. He pleaded for someone to believe him. "I hear the thing ticking...It's gonna go off. I don't have much time! I'm not lying!" he said. After realizing that no one was buying his story, he became quiet and unusually calm. Some say he resigned himself to dying after realizing that no one believed his story.

*The first passion of a successful adult life is a passion for God.*

After a brief struggle, as if trying to free himself from the bomb, Brian made one last plea. "This isn't me," he said, "Did you call my boss?" At 3:18 PM, with news cameras rolling, the bomb exploded. It blew a fist-sized hole in Brian's chest and took his life seconds later.

Brian's family believes that he was a victim, but investigators have never been able to solve the crime. Brian Well's final moments of life remain a mystery. I believe the people who *knew* him. They say that Brian was no mystery—he could have never been a part of such a crime.

Bizarre. What does a man do with a bomb locked around his neck and a world that won't believe his story? Brian Wells was in a no-win situation.

Here's my point: many young adults view surrender to God as a no-win situation—about as appealing as strapping on a bomb. We see *God* as the threat rather than our own *ignorance*. In actuality, life is the other way around.

You entered life with a bomb strapped to your chest—a sin nature—bent toward self-destruction. Jesus said it this way, "...wide is the gate, and broad is the way, that leadeth to destruction, and many there be which go in thereat" (Matthew 7:13). Without God's intervention, you were *going* to blow yourself up—it was just a matter of time. You *would have* chosen the wrong path.

The only thing that could have saved Brian Well's life would have been a personal friendship with someone on the bomb squad. If someone *with the power to help* had known him *personally*, things could have been different. Even so, the only person who can free you from a life of eternal worthlessness is the God who has the power to *free* you into His will. Knowing God isn't bondage! *Not* knowing God is bondage!

To the degree that you are close to God, you are empowered by Him to live the fullest life. To the degree that you neglect Him, you are in bondage to your own susceptibility to sin. People who know God trust Him. People who trust God submit to Him. People who submit to God live abundantly—they win!

The first passion of a successful adult life—a life of big rewards—is *a passion for God*. You could go through life ignoring Him, restricting Him to emergencies, or walking closely with Him! Why settle for less when the throne-room of Heaven and the huge heart of God is extended towards you? Enter in and enjoy the presence of the King!

We've seen eight principles about developing intimacy with God.

---

**A close relationship with God:**
1. *Begins by birth*
2. *Is structured but not systematic*
3. *Is developed through time*
4. *Requires transparency*
5. *Strengthens through commitment*
6. *Solidifies through trust*
7. *Becomes intimate through exclusivity*
8. *Thrives on submission*

---

Remember my friend, Joe, who told me that life is scary? He learned this relationship, just as I did—in the midst of pressure. Early in his college days, he was overwhelmed by the odds that were stacked against him. He didn't have much family support for his Christian walk, and the devil often tempted him to retreat and reconsider his options. In these times of doubt Joe would find his way to my office or to my home to discuss the turmoil. We spent many late hours at local restaurants together. I've never seen a more intense soul struggle.

Over and over again I urged Joe to go to God. I told him to find a quiet place, take a long walk, and pour his heart out to God. God was the only one who could give him the spiritual strength, and the clarity that he really needed.

I could almost pinpoint the day that Joe finally took me up on my counsel. He stopped drowning his sorrows in laughter, video games, TV, and friends, and started taking them to God. It was obvious to me because his countenance was different. His demeanor had changed. He had developed a root system in a relationship with God. Maturity, courage, confidence, and steadfastness grew where doubt once resided.

Joe had opened the door to Abba. He had supped. And everything else turned out to be okay. Time with God changes you. Time with God strengthens you. Being close to God puts life in a fresh perspective—a truthful perspective.

Time after time, Satan will distort life's perspective and attempt to get you off course. If God is your *anchor*, you'll never drift too far. If He is your *refuge*, you'll never have to run! Time with God lifts the fog. Time with God brings Satan's distortions back into perspective. Time with God settles your heart, straightens your course, and strengthens your life.

God knows how to diffuse every bomb in Satan's arsenal!

Get *passionate* about growing close to Him!

## CHAPTER ELEVEN

# A PASSION FOR GOD'S PERFECT WILL—PART ONE

*Embracing God's Purpose*

Psychologist Jeffrey Arnett made an insightful statement in the TIME article. He said of the twixter generation, "They're not just looking for a job. They want something that's more like a calling, that's going to be an expression of their identity." The article didn't provide any answers for finding that calling or uncovering that identity, but God does.

What do you want to do with your life? Perhaps you don't know and that's why you're reading this book. Most likely, if you inspect your heart, you will find dreams—some recent, some distant. If you dig deep, you will uncover desires that have long been alive in your heart.

The good thing about these desires is that God placed them within you. They are His fingerprints in your heart. The bad thing about these desires is that they can become gods unto themselves. Desires make terrible gods. But good desires in God's hands can become a wonderful destiny!

Secular culture sends you on a process of "self-discovery." That's like sending my six-year-old daughter on a road-trip—by herself! It's not going to be fun. It's going to be lonely, scary, and dangerous. A process of self-discovery is empty and disappointing. As one woman said, "I finally got in touch with my inner self, and she's just as confused as I am!" When you finally discover yourself, you'll find out you don't really have much to offer yourself! *Self* makes a terrible god.

There are a couple of real problems with following your desires—a couple of big reasons you should be very wary.

***First, your desires could be misleading you and setting you up for major disappointment.*** Do you realize how many people do what they *want* to do only to discover that they don't *really want* that? Your future desires are based upon your imagination. You have imagined what the fulfillment of those desires might be like. And your imagination is far more generous than reality, so when you finally get what you think you *want*, it's not what you *imagined*! It's not what you *expected*. Your desires set you up for disappointment and drop you hard!

***Second, your desires will change.*** I hate to tell you this, but desires are emotional—they fluctuate. They are fluid. They develop, emerge, grow, and morph. Sometimes they flat do a U-turn. As your life experiences change, so do your desires. In some sense they evolve based upon your personal development. Therefore, if you follow them, you will forever be changing course and "starting over." It's silly that some people would tell you to "follow your heart."

Have you ever seen a bat fly? They forever change course. They dart back and forth like crazed rodents.

Sometime ago, I was sitting in my office on a Sunday morning quietly preparing my Sunday school lesson. Out of the corner of my eye, I noticed something flying over my right shoulder. At first I thought it was a moth of some kind.

Another quick glance caused me to pause. I thought to myself, that's some kind of *huge* moth! At that point, I whipped my chair around only to see a nasty, black bat zinging right for my head. Naturally I ducked, but that didn't help. He passed quickly overhead, and shot right back at me from the front. Once again, I ducked.

At this point, my most terrifying fifteen seconds in ministry took place. That bat wouldn't give up. He circled, dodged, wove, and dove—every time he was aiming straight for my head! I'm already losing my hair, so I didn't need this! They didn't cover this in Bible college!

In frantic panic, I was ducking, dodging, weaving, and waving. I'm grabbing things off my desk and throwing them at him—first a music book, then a CD, then some papers. I'm shouting, "Whoa...yikes...uh-oh...ho..." with punctuated inflection as if the vocal expression was somehow helping. In a last dash for freedom, I jumped around the corner of my desk, hovered low, and dove out of my office—narrowly missing his last kamikaze dive for my scalp.

My office door had been cracked by about six inches, and a good friend was standing just outside—eyes wide, jaw dropped—marveling. All he saw were books flying and arms flailing. He heard my shouts. He thought I was in a fight with someone.

"Dude, there's a bat in my office!" I said, trying to catch my breath.

We had a good laugh. A few moments later, another friend bagged the bat, which had landed under my desk, and the next day our fifth grade science class learned firsthand about one of God's nastiest creatures.

Your desires, apart from God, can be about as erratic as that bat! Following your heart is like trying to swat a fly—it's unpredictable. By following your heart or your desires, you will live in a constant state of experimentation. It's time to stop experimenting and start living.

Dr. Arnett said it well—deep in your heart you desire a life calling that connects with your identity. I have just two questions. If we believe that a person can have a "life calling"—whom do we believe is calling? And whom do we believe created or designed such a specific "identity"? I thought we were just randomly evolved biological matter? Ground beef doesn't have a life calling or an identity—and that's all that evolution says you are! Secular culture really is the blind leading the blind.

You *do* desire a *life's calling*—God put that in you because He has a calling for you! You also have a very intricate identity—you are unique. Your gifts, abilities, interests, experiences, and personality make you one-of-a-kind!

Let me bring you in on a secret. The most incredible life you ever imagined is when your life's calling meets your unique identity. When *who* you are meets *why* you are—WHAM!—life suddenly goes to a new level and becomes "out-of-this-world" awesome! Here's another secret—both can only be discovered in God. He's the designer and builder. He has the blueprints. Only He knows *how* you are built and *why* you are built!

To really enjoy successful adulthood, you must become passionate about discovering and living out *who* you are (your unique identity) and *why* you are (your life's calling). But here's the catch: you can only do so with God. It's like a hidden treasure, and God has the only map! If you don't go to Him, you'll never find it!

When you hear the words, "God's perfect will for your life" this is what we're talking about. God's will is simply the fullest expression of *who* you are combined with *why* you are. Don't get scared by the term "will of God." It's simply what you already long for deep within your heart! If you run from God's will, you run from your truest self—the fullest expression of who God created you to be!

# If I Were Me

A couple of months ago, we enjoyed an awesome family vacation in Florida. During that vacation, we were celebrating my son Lance's fifteenth birthday. Unfortunately, we had shopped for him *before* vacation and had left his birthday gifts at home. Not wanting to be cruddy parents, we decided to take Lance to the mall to pick out a couple of small gifts. On the way there, we began an amusing discussion about what he should choose as his gifts. We were each inserting our own two-cents-worth into the discussion.

I started by saying, "If I were you, I'd get...."

After I filled in the blank, my younger son Larry piped up, "Well, if I were you, I would..." and he proceeded to fill in the blanks.

Dana was starting to feel left out of the conversation, so at that point she said, "Well, *if I were me...*" and then she paused.

And at that, the rest of the family fell apart! We made fun of her for the next thirty minutes. In fact, we've made fun of her for the past two months!

I have to tell you—that statement struck me as more than just funny. As I've prayed about this chapter, it keeps coming back to mind—*if I were me.*

Do you realize that a lot of people live their whole lives and never discover who they really are? (And apparently my wife is one of them!) They never live out the unique design of God for their lives. They never truly discern who God created them to be and what He created them to do.

A lot of people will stand in eternity and say, "If only I were me!" "If only I had yielded to God and lived the life He created for me!"

You don't have to do that.

To enjoy the rewards of adult life, you must become passionate about discovering and doing the perfect will of God. You must become obsessed with discovering your life's calling and doing it to the fullest of your unique identity.

You must get fanatical about discovering your true destiny. It doesn't involve *experimentation*. It involves *sanctification*—surrender to God. It doesn't involve *self-discovery*. It involves *God-discovery*. It doesn't involve a *perpetual state of limbo*. It involves a *continual state of seeking and following*.

God's will is the point where divinely authored circumstances lead you to the combination of your calling, your gifts, your desires, your purpose, your unique design, and God's eternal purpose. It is where all of these things reach critical mass!

The really scary thing is, if you don't get *passionate* about it, you could miss it.

## God's Extravagance vs. My Feeble Imagination

Many young adults are scared to death of these two words—*God's will*. Let me ask you, are you scared of the following words? *Surprise birthday party! Summer vacation! Christmas morning! Graduation gift!* If you are, then you need more help than I can give you. Please set this book down and immediately check yourself into the nearest psych ward.

When I see Christian adults fear God's will, I want to check them into a spiritual psych ward. They misunderstand something. Somehow a connection isn't being made. How could you possibly fear a meeting between your *desires* and your *Designer*? Why would you prevent the meeting of *how* you are made with *why* you are made? How could your thinking be so deceived and convoluted? You might as well spend your life chasing bats!

Quit trusting your imagination and start trusting God's Word. You probably never realized this, but God never speaks of the human imagination in a good light. Check it out for yourself. In Scripture, the human imagination is mentioned every time as lying, deceiving, and misleading. God says to cast it down. He says it is vain and mischievous. He says it is evil continually. To imagine means "to fabricate and sometimes in a malicious sense." In other words, God isn't interested in the artificial fabrications of our imagination, and He warns us not to give them heed or follow them because they are malicious. He warns us to take them hostage and remove them from power in our lives. "Casting down imaginations, and every high thing that exalteth itself against the knowledge of God, and bringing into captivity every thought to the obedience of Christ" (2 Corinthians 10:5).

In contrast, 1 Corinthians 2:9 says, "But as it is written, Eye hath not seen, nor ear heard, neither have entered into the heart of man, the things which God hath prepared for them that love him." God doesn't have an imagination. He deals in reality—truth—and His reality is so extravagant that it can't even enter into our human reasoning.

God's perspective for your future is not an *imagination*—it's a *vision*. God specializes in *vision*. The biblical word *vision* refers to a revealed mental picture. When God places a vision into your heart, it's not a malicious fabrication; it's an *eventual reality* if you will trust Him. Imagination is *man*-centered. Vision is *God*-centered. Imagination flows from *malice*. Vision flows from *purity*. "Blessed are the pure in heart: for they shall see God" (Matthew 5:8). Imagination is *fabricated*. Vision is *revealed*. Imagination is *false*. Vision is God-given, *eventual truth*. Imagination initiates in the deceptive *human heart*. Vision originates with *God's Word*. Proverbs 29:18 says, "Where there is no vision, the people perish: but he that keepeth the law, happy is he."

Imaginations are to be *cast down*. Vision from God is to be *obeyed*. "Whereupon, O king Agrippa, I was not disobedient unto the heavenly vision" (Acts 26:19).

Imaginations are dangerous because they are lies—larger-than-life—so we merely set ourselves up for disappointment. But God's reality—God's vision—is far more extravagant than life as we *imagine*. It's more extravagant than anything we can fabricate.

You can reject God's will and follow your lying imagination to disappointed reality, or you can embrace God's will and follow His vision to extravagant reality— abundant life!

Read that again. It's really important!

If you follow your imagination, it's a dead-end road with a bunch of guys waiting to tie a bomb around your neck. It's a lie with a death wish at the end. It's a darting bat, and it's anybody's guess where it will land. If you follow God, you're dealing with extravagant vision—*eventual reality*. You're opting for the best life—the fusing together of your calling and your identity. And you can be sure it will land you in the center of your unique, eternal purpose. There's no guesswork or experimentation with God's will—only delightful, extravagant truth. Now that's a great life!

## Commitment to God's Call and Purpose

Successful adulthood requires a commitment to discovering God's call on your life. Our American culture doesn't mind commitment as long as you're committing to the wrong things. For instance, Satan would rather you commit to a cell phone provider than to God. He would rather you obsess over text messaging than developing purpose in life. He would rather you commit to casual sex than to Christ. He would rather you sign the dotted line of a car purchase than a ministry call.

Let me be frank. To experience God's best, you must commit to His will more than anything else in life. His plan must become your first passion—His purpose, your first priority. Everything else in your life—from your job to your dating relationships to your friends to your fun— must become subservient to this passionate pursuit. God is a rewarder, but He is conditional in that promise. He plays favorites. He rewards "them that diligently seek him" (Hebrews 11:6).

I've seen a lot of young people who were obsessed with personal desires. Even good desires can becomes idols when they are pursued in place of God.

Desires apart from God are unreliable and insignificant. Desires paired with God's will are a force to be reckoned with. Desires fulfilled in God's time and God's way are unbelievably gratifying to the heart. You can follow your desires only to lose them, or you can follow God only to see Him fulfill your desires. It's a paradox—seems absurd, but still true!

There are hundreds of lives and stories that come to mind, but one that I want to share. His name is Clark. He visited our church with his family years ago as a junior in high school. He was and still is a superb musician—the best violist I've ever heard. At seventeen, he had plans and dreams. He wasn't all that interested in God's will, but God was interested in him. God put on my heart to try to connect with Clark. I tried for several months to get him to come to my class or to youth activities. He just wasn't interested. When he finally came, he sat in the back of class, stayed quiet, and tried not to connect with anyone.

Over time, God worked on Clark's parents. They became faithful, growing members of our church, which meant that Clark was stuck coming to my class. He had to. And little by little he opened up—to me and to God.

At that time, Clark was playing his viola in a local band with some friends. They were having fun. But God put on my heart to invite Clark to play in our church orchestra. During a bus ride to In-N-Out Burger one Sunday night after church, I encouraged Clark to quit his band, surrender to God, and use his abilities for his Creator. During this same time, I was teaching the *Discover Your Destiny* material in class. He was getting both barrels.

Clark's heart softened. Just before his senior year, he surrendered to God and literally came alive! He became a spiritual leader in our youth group like few ever have. He fell in love with God and played in the orchestra. Later during his senior year, God called Clark into the ministry. One step at a time, a life course began to unfold that would have never entered into Clark's imagination.

A year later, he began Bible college. A year after that, he met an incredible girl and fell in love. The next year, he was called to missions work in the Philippines. Then he was married and entered the ministry as one of our youth pastors. For two years, Clark and I had the privilege of working side by side. Our wives became co-laborers in the ministry. We became close friends. We saw many victories together.

As a few more years passed, God blessed Clark and his wife, Rachel, with a beautiful baby boy. Then He provided full support for their missions work and gave them a ministry position next to Dr. Rick Martin—in my estimation, one of the greatest missionaries that God has ever given this planet! Now, Clark is living out a new dream. His *identity* has collided with his *calling*, and he is experiencing *destiny*!

The blessings are too numerous to tell! The mere fact that God took this violist and gave him influence over an orchestra of more than seventy members in the Philippines is well beyond what Clark would have ever imagined. A wife and son—both indescribable blessings that would have been non-existent had Clark not trusted God.

If Clark had committed himself to his own desires, he'd probably be playing viola in clubs and still studying some secular career path in a "way off course" college. Who knows where he would have ended up. I once asked him in front of a group of young people what would have happened in his life if he hadn't set aside self and embraced God's will. He just shook his head, teared up, and couldn't really find the words to describe his gratitude to God.

Don't commit to *your* desires. Don't follow *your* dreams. Follow God. His dreams are better, you just don't know it yet! Commit to Christ. Let your dreams die on the altar of God's amazing plan. Let desires get in line behind God's will.

Become fanatical. Fixate on God's will. Let your heart be gripped irreversibly by an obsession to fulfill His unique plan.

Recently, a young man I've spent a lot of counseling hours with became disillusioned with God and began to stray from His will. As of this writing, he hasn't returned yet. I'm praying he soon will. It all began sometime ago when he fell in love. What began as love gradually and almost unnoticeably became selfish obsession. Parents, friends, and pastors alike were in favor of this relationship, but under the surface things were changing.

Over time, some bad decisions were made, some hearts were hurt, and the relationship fell apart. My prayer and hope was that someday, by God's grace, the relationship might make a recovery. I was pulling for both young adults. I wanted them to see God's best blessings for their future.

But there came a moment when that young man began to want *her* more than *God*. He was convinced that God wanted him to have her, though all providential circumstances said otherwise—including the young lady's own words. Rather than attach his heart to the will of God, he abandoned his heart to carnal passion. Rather than wait for the girl that God created for him, he had to have *this* girl *now*. Imagination is a powerful force when it is exalting itself against God.

> *Desires apart from God are unreliable and insignificant.*

Time has told the story. Disillusioned by his own imagination, he has walked away from God. God didn't let him down, imagination did.

Are you pursuing personal desires over God's will? If so, you're playing with a dangerous fire. Extinguish it, and re-throne God. You must commit to God's will before anything else.

In every matter, your heart must be—if it is the will of God, then I will do this or that. "For that ye ought to say, If the Lord will, we shall live, and do this, or that" (James 4:15). God's will comes first, *everything* and *everyone* else takes a back seat—no matter how pretty she is!

## Finding Your Way in God's Will

One of my favorite TIME quotes is this one, "There are few road maps in the popular culture...to get twixters where they need to go." Good luck, twixters! We don't have a clue! Don't you just love secular culture? It makes you wonder what made popular culture so *popular*?

The question I'm asked more than any other is this: how do I know for sure what the will of God is for my life?

First, let me dispel the expectation behind the question. Young adults have a strange expectation in their minds regarding the will of God. It's a funny little game of self-deception that goes like this: God's will is so abstract, so "out-there," so nebulous, that I want Him to tell me upfront exactly what it involves from start to finish. I need to know—RIGHT NOW—because I may not want to do it!

I say it's a weird game because God's will is no more nebulous or "out-there" than anything else in life. Think about this—whether we are *in* or *out* of the will of God, none of us has a clue what tomorrow holds! It's not like we can see the future lived *our way*, but God's will is *hidden* behind curtain number three! There goes imagination again! We *imagine* what our futures might be, we buy into imagination, believe it, and invest our whole hearts into it like it's a guaranteed insurance policy. What a joke! We put more trust in our imaginations than in God's promises!

We actually expect our imaginations to unfold just as we see them. We're kidding ourselves.

Our biggest plans, apart from God, are at best weakly devised imaginations that probably won't turn out anything like we hope or expect. They are *more* abstract than God's will and infinitely *less likely*. Yet somehow, because they are *ours,* we value them—we trust them—we stake *everything* on them.

On the other hand, we believe that God's plans are suspicious, not to be trusted, and will most likely destroy all happiness in our lives. We imagine that God's plans will surely lead us to the jungles of Africa to eat grubs and preach to naked people. After all—look at Clark! He's in the Philippines, isn't he? Yes—because he *wants* to be! He's loving life more now than he ever imagined he would. His calling connected with his identity—and now his heart is abundantly full and his life abundantly blessed. It's a good thing he went with God and cast down imagination—that he traded his agenda for God's!

There is a way to know for sure what God's will is, but not the way most people expect. But if it's any comfort, you can't see the outcome of *your own* plans in advance either. You can hope. You can risk. You can gamble that your plans will work, but you have no guarantee. With God's will, you can have certainty.

Most Christians want God to reveal His entire will at one time—like a proposal waiting to be signed off and approved. But He doesn't work that way. He never has.

Let me tell you a story.

A good friend of mine has a minivan with a GPS system installed. These things are pretty cool. A few years ago, when he first purchased this van, we went out together, and he was excited to show me this GPS system. We got into the car, entered an address and suddenly the car "binged" and a beautiful, female voice said, "Proceed out of the parking lot and turn left on 40th Street East." This woman sounded so nice, I doubt my wife would even let me have one of these things! (I'm sure Dana would have said that there was a hint of flirtatiousness in her voice.)

We proceeded out of the parking lot and turned left. Then nothing. For more than a mile, the voice was silent. I waited. I listened. Nothing. Then, when I was just about to give up hope, the car "binged" again, and the voice said, "Approaching Avenue K, please turn right in one quarter of a mile."

At this point my friend smiled and said, "Watch this." He did the unthinkable! He went straight. He disobeyed the nice lady in the speaker. "Bing!" "You missed your turn. Please turn around and turn left on Avenue K." She wasn't angry. She just tried to immediately intervene and remind him that he missed the instruction.

My stubborn friend said, "Watch this..." and he disobeyed again. He just kept going straight. This time the voice came back on with a new set of instructions. Based on our current position, the nice female computer had rerouted our course to get us back on target for the destination, "Bing... approaching Avenue M, please turn right." My friend just smiled with warm satisfaction, as if to say, "I bet you don't have a car that does this!"

This thing—or this lady—was pretty cool. She never lost her temper. She just persistently, consistently tried to tell us where to go. Between instructions she was silent. When it was time to make a turn, she spoke up again. She never left us hanging and never misled us. And when we disobeyed, she rerouted us and made every effort to get us back on course.

God leads like GPS.

There's another way of finding your way around in this high-tech world. It's called MapQuest. MapQuest is pretty cool too, but it's very different. When you go to *mapquest.com*, you type in an address, and MapQuest calculates every step of the journey down to the tenth of a mile. It tells you A–Z exactly what to do and where to go, all in one set of instructions. You can read it, print it, take it with you, and know exactly what exits, what turns, and what distance you will travel. Every small detail is spelled out in advance.

God isn't like MapQuest.

When it comes to God's will, we want MapQuest. We want to know for sure every step of the quest from start to finish. We want to visit God's mapquest.com and get a printout of the whole plan upfront.

But God wants to give us GPS—one step at a time with long periods of silence in between. When you disobey, He will intervene and try to get you back on course. When you ignore His warnings and end up where you're not supposed to be, He will reroute your life back into His will, but He does so one instruction at a time. GPS. Not MapQuest.

Stop asking for MapQuest. Punch in the destination— God's perfect will—and then obey one command at a time. He will let you know exactly what to do when you need to do it. You'll know in your heart! He will confirm it through His Word, through circumstances, through prayer, through counsel, and through godly authority. You won't know *everything* in advance, but you will know *what to do next.* Do it. There will never be a time when He will not guide you into His perfect will, as long as you are passionate about seeking!

This is big stuff, and you need a break. We've only started this subject of God's perfect will. There's a bit more to say about it in the next chapter. Proceed when you are ready, and until then chew on this stuff for a while. See you in part two when you can stomach it.

# CHAPTER TWELVE

# A PASSION FOR GOD'S PERFECT WILL—PART TWO

*Embracing God's Purpose*

In the last chapter we explored God's extravagance. We defined God's perfect will—when *who* you are meets *why* you are. We saw the need to commit passionately—to *obsess* over doing the will of God, and we discovered that God leads more like GPS than MapQuest.

Finding and living God's will is a one-decision-at-a-time process. At times it can seem painfully vague, but He will never leave you instruction-less when it's time to move forward. He has an amazing way of making circumstances work out perfectly to bring about His purpose in your life. That's what makes Him God.

> And we know that all things work together for good to them that love God, to them who are the called according to his purpose.—ROMANS 8:28

## An Awesome Love Story of God's Leading

In Genesis 24, Abraham sent his servant (most likely Eliezer) to find a wife for his son. He sent him to his hometown because he wanted a bride from among his own people. Finding a bride for your master's son—now that's some serious responsibility. In Genesis 24:12 Eliezer said, "O LORD God of my master Abraham, I pray thee, send me good speed this day, and shew kindness unto my master Abraham." To tackle this enormous responsibility, he turned to God. He prayed that God would reveal His will and guide him for the sake of his master. He asked the Lord specifically to show him the right girl, and expected to wait until the Lord would answer his prayer.

But the Bible says, "And it came to pass, before he had done speaking, that, behold, Rebekah came..." (Genesis 24:15). God was way ahead of Eliezer. Before he finished his prayer, God answered it. A beautiful story unfolds as Eliezer meets Rebekah's family, tells them of God's leading, and Rebekah chooses to return with Eliezer to become Isaac's wife. It's quite a love story. To save time, let's skip right to the end. This is the best part.

"And Isaac went out to meditate in the field at the eventide: and he lifted up his eyes, and saw, and, behold, the camels were coming. And Rebekah lifted up her eyes, and when she saw Isaac, she lighted off the camel. For she had said unto the servant, What man is this that walketh in the field to meet us? And the servant had said, It is my master: therefore she took a vail, and covered herself. And the servant told Isaac all things that he had done. And Isaac brought her into his mother Sarah's tent, and took Rebekah, and she became his wife; and he loved her: and Isaac was comforted after his mother's death" (Genesis 24:63–67). Isaac was *spending time* with God; Rebekah was *obeying* God and suddenly, it was love at first sight, and for the rest of their lives! Isn't God great!

There are many principles about God's will in this wonderful love story. Though Rebekah and Isaac had never before met each other, God led them directly to each other. That sure beats dating services, singles hangouts, and bar hopping! God really does know what He's doing with your life.

God surpassed both Rebekah's and Isaac's dreams by bringing them together. Both were more focused on living right than they were with finding a spouse. Both were living lives of honor to God and authority. Here are a few more principles:

***God's will involves being in God's way.*** We see Eliezer leaving home with nothing more than a vision of what could be. He was utterly dependent upon God's guidance, and he was following GPS-like instructions. When offering Rebekah's family an explanation of God's leading, here's what he said, "Blessed be the LORD God of my master Abraham, who hath not left destitute my master of his mercy and his truth: I being in the way, the LORD led me…" (Genesis 24:27).

Eliezer simply made sure he was "in God's way." He made sure he was heading God's direction—the *guidance* was up to God. He was secure in "not knowing" because he knew that *God* knew. When you're holding God's hand, you don't have to wonder where to go next. You just keep walking as He leads.

***God's will sometimes involves seasons of silence.*** In this case, God spoke immediately, but that's not how He always works. Sometimes there is an agonizing waiting period between the first moment you begin praying about direction and the time that God finally reveals His leading. You might pray for years about a spouse only to have God's silence in return. You might seek His will for months in a matter before He gives you any guidance. Don't let this frustrate you. Expect it.

During these times of silence the devil wants you to rush into your own decisions. He wants you to *preempt* God. When God is silent, simply *wait* until He speaks. Don't panic. Don't worry and fret. Just continue seeking. He will never take His eyes off you. Psalm 32:8 says, "I will instruct thee and teach thee in the way which thou shalt go. I will guide thee with mine eye."

***God's will requires a listening heart.*** There are a few key ways that God speaks, and all of them are seen in this story.

First and foremost, He speaks through *His Word*. Abraham was following the commands of God in selecting a wife for Isaac. He was seeking a wife from his own kindred. Even so, you must have a listening heart to the Word of God, and His Word must be the *final authority* in your life.

Second, He speaks through *godly authority*. He will use the guiding voices of parents, pastors, and others to give you wisdom and guidance. Eliezer was following the instructions of his master, and God blessed. He had a submissive heart to God-given authority and God honored him for it. We'll see the importance of this again in a moment.

Third, He speaks through *circumstances*. Eliezer had a wise heart to see God's hand in circumstances. What others may have taken as casual happenstance, Eliezer saw as divine providence. Every circumstance of your life has a *divine blueprint* to it. Do you look for God's guidance in the circumstances? Do you ask, "Lord, what are you trying to say to me here? What do I need to learn?" There may be some circumstances, large or small, in your life right now that will take on a different light the moment you ask God to open your eyes.

Fourth, He speaks through His *still small voice within*. His Holy Spirit will always confirm His will in your heart. The question is, are you sensitive to that small voice, or have you quenched it? Eliezer knew that God had led him. He confirmed it personally through prayer.

Fifth, He speaks through *godly counsel*. Eliezer told his whole story to Rebekah's family—her godly authorities, and everybody on *both* sides of the family confirmed that this was the will of God. God was working in everybody's heart! We're going to talk about this more in a moment.

When you are *listening* to God, remember that He speaks in these five ways. Most importantly, remember that His Word is the litmus test for all other speaking. His Word is the final authority. The leading of God will *never* contradict His Word.

## Establishing a Biblical Decision Process

Have you ever considered how much guesswork goes into life-changing decisions for most people? It's flat scary. Slogans like "follow your dreams, do it your way, discover yourself, and if it feels good, do it" leave you dangling from the thread of your "best guess." Long ago, I decided I didn't want to live life according to my best guess. I wanted God's best—period.

I'm shocked at how many Christian young adults sink into this mentality. You need to know something. God doesn't want you to GUESS about anything in life! He doesn't want you making *one* decision by guesswork. He wants you to have full assurance—*certainty*. He wants you to *know* that you *know* you're doing the right thing! He wants your decisions to be well-made—confident in Him. And once they are made, He wants no second-guessing.

If you live life your way, your best approach to decision-making will be the "pros and cons" method. You'll weigh the possibilities, the risks, and the benefits of all your options, and then you'll make your guess. Of the tens of thousands of colleges, careers, and locations you could choose, you will weigh out the options and ultimately throw a dart into the darkness of decision-making. You have no way of peering into the future and seeing the outcome. You'll just guess.

In contrast, God wants your decisions to be backed by solid truth, verifiable leading, and confirmable proof that you are doing His will. He wants to establish your decisions in the bedrock of His guidance. He wants you to be sure of what you're doing and why you're doing it. It's not guesswork. It's *certainty* based upon God's verifiable leading.

In *Discover Your Destiny* I wrote about a biblical process of decision-making. I cannot rehearse it all in these pages, but I would remind you that God isn't into pros and cons. For your decisions to last and bear fruit, you must have a biblical process in making decisions. You must be able to verify God's leading and look back at His guidance.

Every right decision in your life will be questioned by Satan and tested by circumstances. Well-made decisions withstand these tests like gold withstands fire. Well-made decisions are like well-built buildings. The foundation that goes deep doesn't collapse in strong winds or storms. Even so, the decision that is undergirded by a strong foundation will withstand the tests and fires of life.

Well-made decisions are strong. Every decision you make should be strong.

Let me give a personal example. I've never had to wonder if I'm doing God's will with my life. I've never had to wonder if I married the right person. Why? Because when I was a young adult, I didn't trust myself, and subjected my decisions to biblical tests. I went to great effort to verify that my choices were God's choices—proving them through prayer, God's Word, and godly counsel. There's no need to question them. They stand strong because they were decided biblically.

It's not that the devil hasn't tested them. It's not that he hasn't tempted me to reconsider. It's that every time he does, his temptation is ridiculous. I can remember those moments when these decisions were made. I can remember the leading of God. I recall how prayerfully and cautiously they were made. These decisions are grounded firmly in the bedrock of God's guidance.

A biblical process of decision-making will provide this bedrock confidence in your own life. Your decisions must be strong. Making decisions quickly, prayerlessly, haphazardly, or emotionally will only guarantee that these decisions are weak and fragile.

Would you like to know why so many people can't keep a commitment? Frankly, their decision-making process is riddled with holes. They dive headfirst into major, life-altering decisions without having a strong basis for the decision! Their decisions, when tested, are easily questioned because their process of decision-making was weak to begin with.

Popular culture's way of making a decision is more like flipping a coin, reading a fortune cookie, or calling the psychic hotline. God's way of decision-making is verifiable, certain, and strong. Go with God.

## What To Do with a Conflict of Wills

Have you ever had a conflict of wills with a person?

Haylee is one of two strong-willed children in our family, and one of the biggest battles of wills we've ever had was at a swimming pool. She was three, and I was thirty-four. I was standing in three feet of water, arms stretched towards her, telling her to come to me, but she wouldn't. Strong-willed and defiant, she stood on the side of the pool. She was decked out in floaties, goggles, a pretty pink swimsuit, and an attitude to match—and she refused to budge. She didn't trust me, and she wasn't about to obey me.

The more she refused, the more resolute I became. A standoff had begun, and she wasn't giving in. Finally, I stepped out of the pool, scooped her up into my arms, and carried her into the water. She was kicking and screaming the whole way, but since that time Haylee has become a lover of swimming. My will won that day, and her will died; but over time, a new will was born in her heart. It was a painful process for both of us, but worth the effort.

Have you ever had a battle of wills with God? The difference is, He won't *force* you to submit. He will allow you to resist Him. You really don't want a battle of the wills with God, because He will let you win—in which case, you lose.

A *battle* of wills must never happen between you and God, but a *conflict* of wills is inevitable.

Jesus never had a battle of wills with His Heavenly Father. "Jesus saith unto them, My meat is to do the will of him that sent me, and to finish his work" (John 4:34). "For I came down from heaven, not to do mine own will, but the will of him that sent me" (John 6:38). For Jesus to battle with His Heavenly Father would have been sin. This never happened.

But He *did* have a *conflict* of wills. In other words, there was a time when Jesus' human will didn't line up with His Father's will. There was a time when He was required to set aside *His* will for His *Father's*. He never resisted. He never fought His Father's will. But He did desire things to be different. Just before He went to Calvary, He prayed these words, "Father, if thou be willing, remove this cup from me..." (Luke 22:42). He was surely asking that things be different. We know there was a conflict of wills because of what He said next, "...nevertheless not my will, but thine, be done." He set aside His will for His Father's.

What can we learn from this?

***First, if Jesus had a conflict of wills, you will too.*** There will be moments when *your* will doesn't line up with *God's*. You should expect this. It is a normal part of the human relationship with God, and it doesn't have to become disobedience or defiance.

Sometimes we ignore the conflict and pretend it doesn't exist. This is when the *conflict* of wills becomes a *battle* of wills. Deep within, these battles rob our peace and bring unrest to our soul. You will never be a more miserable Christian than when you are fighting God's will in your life. Don't let the *conflict* become a *battle.*

**Second, let God change your will through surrender.** When you let your will die, God does something supernatural within you. He *changes* your will. He replaces it with new desires. Just as Jesus' death had to precede His resurrection, even so the death of your will must precede the birth of a new one.

Pray the prayer of Jesus, "...nevertheless not my will, but thine, be done." Wave the white flag of your heart instantly and reflexively. Remember, submission is reflexive obedience.

Clark didn't go to the Philippines against his will. He simply allowed God to direct his will, and now he's having the time of his life!

## Develop a Support Team in Decision-Making

Eliezer didn't venture into his responsibility alone. He knew it was bigger than he was, and so he built a support team. He wasn't out to prove his *individuality*; he was out to find God's will. He wanted *truth.* He refused to trust himself and chose to rely upon God, Abraham, and Rebekah's family. To find the will of God, you must do the same—build a support team for good decisions.

In 1990, Chris McCandless was twenty-two years old. He had grown up in an upper-middle class family, graduated from both high school and college, and seemingly had everything going for him. In spite of his good fortune, he was empty inside and without meaning and direction in life. He longed for that life calling that connected with his identity. He entered his twenties long on questions and short on answers. He had a deep-seated contempt for popular culture and materialism, and he knew there was more to life than cars, computers, and fun. Without a biblical life view, he turned to the wrong place for answers.

In confusion and disappointment he launched out on a misguided process of self-discovery. After college graduation, he changed his name to Alexander Supertramp, gave his $25,000 life savings to charity, and hit the road. He lived by the seat of his pants, traveling across the country, finding odd jobs, withdrawing from society for long periods of time, and generally barely getting by. He had cut off contact with family and friends in search of something much bigger.

In April of 1992, he hitchhiked to Alaska where he dreamed of retreating into the wilderness alone to live off the land and journal his days away. A man named James Gallien dropped him off at the Stampede Trail after giving him a ride from Fairbanks. James offered to help him buy equipment and to properly prepare for his odyssey, but Chris declined. With little in the way of forethought or planning, he hiked alone into the wilds of Alaska. He carried a ten-pound bag of rice, a hunting rifle, some ammunition, some basic camping equipment, and a few books.

Twenty miles into the wilderness, Chris discovered an abandoned bus and set up camp. This became his home for the next five months. During that time, he lived off local plant life and local game. With no experience as a hunter, he even shot a moose, but with no ability to preserve meat, it didn't matter.

Chris's journal covered his experiences over 113 days of living alone in the wild. But his fate began to change toward the end of those entries. That August, Chris decided to hike out of the wilderness, but the trail was blocked by the overflowing Teklanika River at that time of year.

On September 2, 1992, some hikers and hunters found a note that Chris had written posted on the door of the bus. It said, "S.O.S. I need your help. I am injured, near death, and too weak to hike out of here. I am all alone; this is no joke. In the name of God, please remain to save me. I am out collecting berries close by and shall return this evening. Thank you, Chris McCandless." The note was dated some time in August.

The hunters discovered Chris dead in his sleeping bag inside the bus. He had been dead for more than two weeks and the official cause of death was starvation. Isn't it interesting that at the end of his life Chris brought God into it? Why do we always save God for the last minute emergencies?

There are a couple of theories on Chris's death. None of them matter much—he's still dead. Bottom line, Chris died of ignorance. He ate the wrong foods, became ill, and was then too weak to sustain himself. He left home, became the lone-twixter, rode off into the sunset in search of life, and only found death.

Chris was a lost twenty-something kid who didn't know where to turn for answers. Family had let him down. College had too. Friends and fun didn't fill the void either. He was more acutely aware of the vanity of life than most people his age, and he refused to turn to music and parties to drown out the yearnings of his heart.

Ultimately, Chris died because he decided to go it alone in life. He cut off every support structure—and why not? They certainly had let him down on the big questions. He refused to listen to anyone. He had something to prove. He even refused the help of the last man to see him alive. He died in the summer, twenty miles from a well-traveled highway, because he didn't take advice.

As you journey into God's will, you are entering a narrow path, but it is well traveled. Chris thought he was really roughing it. Let's get real. You don't find a bus in virgin wilderness! On your own journey, there are many people who have traveled this same spiritual path. They have passed through the trials, made the decisions, survived the tests, and they stand ready to help.

You can be like Eliezer and rely on the wisdom and guidance of others, or you can be like Chris and essentially self-destruct. You can call on the wisdom of godly people, or you can retreat into your own pride and do things your way. The first is extremely wise and safe. The second is extremely stupid.

People who survive the wilderness of decision-making don't hike alone. They refuse to face life-changing decisions by themselves. And I'm not only talking about young people. I'm talking about wise people of *any* age! Those who make wise decisions know an awesome secret about decision-making. Godly counselors make for safe decisions.

Wise people of every age have a decision-cabinet. They select a group of godly people to surround them. These are like the President's advisors. They provide insight, advice, direction, and verification. They create a strong support system for formulating strong decisions.

Listen to what God says:

> Without counsel purposes are disappointed: but in the multitude of counsellors they are established. —PROVERBS 15:22

> For by wise counsel thou shalt make thy war: and in multitude of counsellors there is safety.—PROVERBS 24:6

> Thy testimonies also are my delight and my counsellors. —PSALM 119:24

> Where no counsel is, the people fall: but in the multitude of counsellors there is safety.—PROVERBS 11:14

You must build a strong support team for your decisions. Don't be the "lone-twixter" of decision-making! Even the Lone Ranger had Tonto. People who go it alone die alone.

As you face your future, one of the wisest things you can do is select a group of people that you believe to be godly, wise, and living in the will of God. Choose people that you believe will shoot straight with you and confront you with the truth. Commit to never making a major decision without consulting and listening to their biblical counsel.

Go to these people and draw out their wisdom. The Bible says, "Counsel in the heart of man is like deep water; but a man of understanding will draw it out" (Proverbs 20:5).

Who should be on your support team? Start with your parents and your pastor for sure. From there, perhaps a youth pastor, grandparents, teachers, and other godly people that God has placed in your life.

One way to make a decision very strong is to surround it with wise people. At every decision point, you should have a multitude of godly people saying, "Yes, that's the right thing to do."

When Dana and I were engaged, every authority figure and godly counselor in our lives was in favor of our marriage. That made a strong case! For every decision, you need a strong case—a multitude of good people confirming and approving your decision.

In 1 Samuel 3:8, God is speaking to young Samuel, but Samuel doesn't realize it. "And the LORD called Samuel again the third time. And he arose and went to Eli, and said, Here am I; for thou didst call me. And Eli perceived that the LORD had called the child." Every time God called, Samuel ran to Eli and said, "Here I am." Now, Eli was a fat man who enjoyed his sleep, and after the third time of being awakened, the Bible says, "Eli perceived that the LORD had called the child." Samuel's authority perceived God's voice before Samuel did!

Here's my point. God-given authority will often perceive God's leading in your life before you do. Don't ignore them. Heed them. God has an amazing way of getting *their* attention so He can get *yours*. Sometimes they will look at the same circumstances you're looking at and see something totally different. You're doing yourself a favor to pay attention.

Over the years, there have been a few times I've said to a young person, "I think God wants you to serve Him. Please listen carefully and make sure you aren't missing the signals." I've seen my pastor and others intervene in situations simply because the Lord placed it on their hearts to do so. It's not a *control* issue—it's a *counsel* issue. Wise young hearts are always glad they listened to godly counsel.

Being passionate about God's perfect will means you will be passionate about verifying His will. Don't do anything without godly advice, and when godly advice doesn't seem to make sense, wait and pray—whatever you do, don't go it alone!

> *To experience God's will, you must have a biblical decision-making process.*

After you have sought the Lord through prayer and Bible study, He will speak to your heart. He will lead you in a specific direction. Before you finalize your decision, you must turn to godly counsel. The time between God's leading and your final decision is the time to strengthen the case. Verify your heart. Put it to the test. Make sure you aren't deceiving yourself.

And be very wary when your heart doesn't want to hear what counselors have to say. When you plug your ears to godly counsel, you're exposing folly in your heart.

The second passion of successful adult living is a passion for the perfect will of God. It's bigger than your imagination. It's the full expression of your identity and your life calling—*who* you are and *why* you are. It requires passionate commitment, and you don't get there by MapQuest, but by GPS—one step at a time.

To experience God's will, you must have a biblical decision-making process, a "not-my-will" attitude, and a spiritual cabinet to give you counsel and confirm God's leading.

Chris McCandless didn't have to die. During his last few weeks he desperately regretted being alone in the wild. As you venture forward, you're not alone. The path of God's will is well traveled by joyful and godly people. Don't isolate yourself from them. Call upon them and take advantage of their wisdom and advice.

And as a side note, if you ever hike alone into the Alaskan wilderness, be sure to take a map so you can get back to the people who care about you after you come to your senses! Don't be Alexander Supertramp. Be Eliezer!

## CHAPTER THIRTEEN

# A PASSION TO FINISH MY COURSE

*Embracing Patient Endurance*

The third godly passion of successful adulthood is a passion to finish the course. Anyone can *start* strong, but few *finish* strong. The best rewards of adulthood require passionate persistence—a fiery refusal to quit.

Most young adults of this generation have completely lost this ability. Stick-ability is rare these days. Our culture is driven by a desire for comfort and ease. Our technologies are developed for the sole purpose of making life easier. Our lifestyles are fashioned by convenience and complacency. Our world is consumed with passivity and lethargy. The twixter generation is apathetic—careless. They know little of paying a price, earning their wings, and reaching their potential. "For all seek their own, not the things which are Jesus Christ's" (Philippians 2:21).

We are programmed to expect everything *now*. We get irritated if we wait more than sixty seconds at a drive thru. We get frustrated when our email isn't instant. We hate to wait. We despise work, love three-day weekends, and thank

God for Fridays. We live for pleasure, aim for nothing, and covet everything. We hesitate to commit, second guess every decision, and retreat at the first sign of discomfort. And for all of our conveniences, we're miserable.

One glimpse of American culture would lead you to believe that our life-purposes are comfort and fun. We major on fun and minor on persistence. We overdose on frivolity and flee from sacrifice. We seek comfort without cost, Christianity without a cross, and rewards without responsibility. The *best life* just doesn't work that way.

The "try it and see if it works out for me" mentality haunts us—it is pervasive in popular culture. But passionless living leads to emptiness. With all of our comforts, conveniences, and cordless devices, we pillow our heads at night wondering what life is all about and why we're not happy! Our conscience bears witness against us. We know that life is bigger than self. The knowledge of our hearts reminds us that there is a purpose worth pursuing with all of our might!

The Apostle Paul was passionate! He lived on purpose. He embraced God and embraced life with fiery determination. He pressed forward. He was gripped by his call. He understood his identity, and he seized the day. He lived every day with selflessness, steadfastness, and certainty.

Just before his death, he wrote these last words to Timothy: "But watch thou in all things, endure afflictions, do the work of an evangelist, make full proof of thy ministry. For I am now ready to be offered, and the time of my departure is at hand. I have fought a good fight, I have finished my course, I have kept the faith" (2 Timothy 4:5-7). At the end of his life, Paul was glad for the price he paid. He was passionate about finishing the course that God called him to run. He kept the faith. He endured.

If anyone ever had reasons to quit, Paul did. He had dozens of them! But he refused. He turned his strong will into an asset. He dug in his heels, with pit-bull determination, and never gave up the fight. A twixter he was not! There was no perpetual state of limbo for the Apostle Paul. No process of self-discovery. Just a dogged defiance against double-mindedness! He had a single laser-like focus in life. He gloried in the cross, embraced the burdens, and fought the good fight of faith.

Throughout the New Testament we see Paul's commitment. From his continual reference to himself as a *servant* of Christ, to his beatings and imprisonments for Christ, to his tireless travels and passionate preaching of the cross—we see a man who knew his Christ, knew his calling, and finished his course.

In the final pages of this book, I want to explore four character traits that Paul wrote about—four requirements of

*Shortcuts don't just shorten the distance; they cheapen the gift.*

finishing your course. If you will be a finisher, you must understand what is required. Finishing your course will not be easy, but it will be worth it. Finishing your course will not be effortless or problem free, but it will bring big rewards.

In these final pages, I want to share with you what God taught me over the last ten years. These words are not mine to you, but rather God's to me! I'm simply letting you in on the conversation. I'm going to share with you what God has used to convict me! At this point, I'm inviting you to sit with me and learn from others—namely Jesus and the Apostle Paul.

In many respects, I'm still early in my journey. But I desperately desire to finish my course. Since I was twelve, my greatest fear has been failure—I long to finish strong. I don't want to be a sprinter, spiritually speaking. I want to be a long-distance runner—a marathoner. I'm barely midway through my own course, God willing. Yet, in handing off the baton of adulthood to you, I would be remiss if I didn't challenge you in this area where your culture is so weak.

How did the Apostle Paul finish so strong? What character traits did he have? What principles forged his fixed heart? What values shaped his strong-willed passion to finish? There are several closely related character traits that stand out when I study Paul's life. Pray with me that God will infuse these into your character as we study them together.

## Finishing Requires Patience

The word *patience* in the New Testament speaks of a cheerful, hopeful continuance. Patience continues to do right, with a good attitude, while waiting on God. It's more than merely waiting. It's active. It's positive. It's hanging in there with a great spirit knowing that God is in control.

I hate to break this to you, but God designed life with waiting periods. You've grown up in a world that is frustrated with waiting. Enter—disappointment with God. If I've been trained that waiting is a pain, and God makes me wait—the translation is, God must be a pain! Culture has done you a great disservice in this respect. We have destroyed patience in young hearts. We haven't taught you that anything is worth waiting for.

May I let you in on a secret? The best stuff in life is worth the wait, and shortcuts don't just shorten the distance; they cheapen the gift! For instance, the world tells you to have sex *now*. God says to have patience and wait until marriage. Sex is *worth* the wait, and it *isn't* worth the *risk and loss* involved with *not* waiting! Waiting for sex makes it highly valuable and rewarding. *Not* waiting makes it worthless, pointless, and risky. Sex now will be severely disappointing and damaging. Sex in marriage will be exclusively wonderful for the rest of your life! That's just one example of thousands. God's best blessings come with a built-in patience factor!

God has a lifetime of blessings that He intends to pour into your life, but patience is the key. Patience is the character trait that will take you from here to there—doing right, continually, with a good attitude, until God fulfills the promise. Hebrews 10:36 says it this way, "For ye have need of patience, that, after ye have done the will of God, ye might receive the promise." Patiently doing the will of God comes first—receiving the promise comes later. That's God's method of blessing your life.

God isn't in a hurry. You're never going to speed Him up. He has a deliberate purpose at work in you, and His timetable is fixed. If you let impatience rob your joy and derail your direction, you lose. If you "let patience have her perfect work" you will "be perfect and entire, wanting nothing" (James 1:4). God is more concerned with the work He's doing *in* you than with your *immediate gratification*. He invites you to "let patience have her perfect work"—let patience complete you.

We live in an impatient world, but we serve a faithful God. He calls you to a life of patient hope. Romans 8:25 says, "But if we hope for that we see not, then do we with patience wait for it." There is a sacred delight—a hope—that comes with cheerful patience.

If you desire to finish your course, you must embrace life with great patience. Psalm 1:1–3 says, "Blessed is the man that walketh not in the counsel of the ungodly, nor standeth in the way of sinners, nor sitteth in the seat of the scornful. But his delight is in the law of the LORD; and in his law doth he meditate day and night. And he shall be like a tree planted by the rivers of water, that bringeth forth his fruit in his season; his leaf also shall not wither; and whatsoever he doeth shall prosper."

What is this passage teaching? Patience. God says if you will delight in my Word, and choose right companions, you will grow like a tree. Your roots will grow deep. Your life will grow strong. And in your season, you will bring forth fruit. That's patience! Continue to do right—dig deep roots, grow strong in truth—and in your season, you will bear fruit. The waiting will be worth it!

Another passage that teaches this waiting principle is Galatians 6:7-9, "Be not deceived; God is not mocked: for whatsoever a man soweth, that shall he also reap. For he that soweth to his flesh shall of the flesh reap corruption; but he that soweth to the Spirit shall of the Spirit reap life everlasting. And let us not be weary in well doing: for in due season we shall reap, if we faint not." God is teaching that there's a span of time between planting seeds and reaping a harvest. Don't be weary with well doing—you will reap!

The basic principle here is that farming requires patience, and so does living for God.

A dear lady in our church has a peach orchard. Not long ago, we took our kids out to that orchard to pick some peaches. While we were there, I asked Muriel what it takes to grow a peach tree. I was shocked at her answer.

"Well, if you get a tree that's a year or so old and plant it, you will have to wait five years to reap any fruit from that tree. It will try to grow fruit sooner, but you'll need to pluck the fruit early so the nutrients will stay in the tree and make it strong and healthy. After five years, you'll have a healthy tree ready to bear fruit!"

Five years? Who wants to wait five years to bear fruit when I can go to the grocery store and have it now? That's exactly how God describes your life—like a tree growing healthy and strong. It will one day bear fruit. Don't take shortcuts. Don't try to rush the process. Let patience have her perfect work. Let God make you strong. Let Him strengthen, establish, settle you. His will and His rewards are worth the wait. He promises, "you shall reap if you faint not." Keep doing right with a good attitude. Keep serving with a smile. Harvest will come! Just keep sowing good seeds, and let patience guide your life.

Finishing your course requires patience, but you live in an impatient world. You'll have to swim upstream on this one, but it's well worth it. Let the patience factor guide you to God's best.

## Finishing Requires Contentment

I know what you're thinking. We define these terms in our minds quickly and move on. Believe me, contentment means more than you think it does. Hang with me for a minute.

Contentment isn't merely about not wanting stuff. This isn't about shortening your Christmas list or not wanting that new car you've had your eye on. Contentment is far bigger than that, and you won't finish your course without it.

Paul wrote in Philippians 4:11, "Not that I speak in respect of want: for I have learned, in whatsoever state I am, therewith to be content." Again, Hebrews 13:5 says, "Let your conversation be without covetousness; and be content with such things as ye have: for he hath said, I will never leave thee, nor forsake thee."

Do you know what this word *contentment* means? It means "to be possessed of unfailing strength." When God says, "Let your conversation (your lifestyle) be without covetousness; and be content...." He's saying much more than "stop wanting a new computer." He's saying, "Let me fill you with unfailing strength so that you have no reason to want." This is why the Shepherd wrote, "The LORD is my shepherd; I shall not want" (Psalm 23:1). When God fills your life and your heart, you stop wanting. That word *want* means to be lacking something. It doesn't mean you don't desire something; it means your life isn't *diminished* for not having it! When you are content, you stop living your life from a position of desperation and start living from a position of satisfaction—fullness.

Consider what it would be like to wake up tomorrow morning and not want anything—feeling completely satisfied with your life. Imagine having a heart so full, so content, so abundant and overflowing, that you just don't feel desperate about anything. Wouldn't that be cool?

Now, lift up your head a little and think bigger. Imagine living your whole life from a position of fullness rather than want. We're talking about the difference between a fat man at a Chinese buffet and a starving refugee in the gutter. The first is full and has need of nothing—he is possessed of unfailing strength. The second will eat anything just to survive! One is satisfied—the other is desperate. The difference is God-given contentment.

About a year ago, God gave us a new home. I can honestly say from our hearts, my wife and I didn't "want" this home, in the biblical sense of the word. We desired it, but we certainly weren't lacking. From a position of fullness, God led us into this home. Had we not received it, our lives wouldn't have been diminished in any way!

Most people go through life from a position of *want*. They crave constantly. They feel that they are lacking. They must have more. Every decision is made from a position of emptiness and desperation. Therefore, every decision is like scavenging for food in the gutter. Others, like Paul, discover how to let God fill their hearts. They live life from a position of fullness and satisfaction. They aren't needy. They don't rush into relationships like starving refugees. They don't hop into bed like love scavengers. They don't run from job to job scraping meager helpings of satisfaction from trash bins. They feast at the King's table! They live from a position of fullness. They don't scrape and scavenge. They select. They make wise choices based on full hearts and careful guidance.

How do you eat at a buffet? Do you pile everything you can on the plate as high as you can like a rabid dog? No. You methodically select exactly what you want, and you're in no rush or stress because you know there's plenty more for the taking! No reason to freak out—you have all you could want or need. Paul wrote it this way, "But I have all, and abound: I am full…" (Philippians 4:18).

This is contentment. It changes your whole perspective in life. You're either a refugee spiritually starving through life, or you're a fat man spiritually full in life. Letting contentment grow in your heart is the difference. This kind of contentment only comes from Christ, and it satisfies your life in a way that will sustain you for the long term.

If you desire to finish your course, you're going to need unfailing strength. So, step up to the King's table and let Him fill you! Nothing else in life can be so incredible!

## Finishing Requires Enduring Confidence

This one is awesome! I've been waiting the whole book to get to this! Don't miss it.

In 2 Corinthians 4:7–9 Paul wrote, "But we have this treasure in earthen vessels, that the excellency of the power may be of God, and not of us. We are troubled on every side, yet not distressed; we are perplexed, but not in despair; Persecuted, but not forsaken; cast down, but not destroyed;" Paul is describing two worlds. His outer man is troubled, perplexed, persecuted, and cast down. But there was another world inside. In his heart, things were different! His inner man was "not distressed, not in despair, not forsaken, and not destroyed." Amazing. Though Paul's world was crumbling around him at times, his inner heart was strong—confident. He had a strength that nothing could touch.

He continues a few verses later, in 2 Corinthians 4:16–5:6, "For which cause we faint not; but though our outward man perish, yet the inward man is renewed day by day. For our light affliction, which is but for a moment, worketh for us a far more exceeding and eternal weight of glory; While we look not at the things which are seen, but at the things which are not seen: for the things which are seen are temporal; but the things which are not seen are eternal. For we know that if our earthly house of this tabernacle were dissolved, we have a building of God, an house not made with hands, eternal in the heavens. For in this we groan, earnestly desiring to be clothed upon with our house which is from heaven: If so be that being clothed we shall not be found naked. For we that are in this tabernacle do groan, being burdened: not for that we would be unclothed, but clothed upon, that mortality might be swallowed up of life. Now he that hath wrought us for the selfsame thing is God, who also hath given unto us the earnest of the Spirit. Therefore we are always confident, knowing that, whilst we are at home in the body, we are absent from the Lord."

*Christ-based confidence compels us forward through resistance.*

The word *confident* in the New Testament refers to a settled inward certainty that rests the soul. It also refers to an outspoken, public assurance. In other words, this is something that comes from Christ and starts in the heart, and then it becomes obvious to others. This is the strength to endure through an inward confidence in Christ. This is knowing that there is a great prize, and then keeping your eyes on that prize. This is what makes the world sit up and take notice. Culture craves this but doesn't know where to get it. God wants you to endure the battles of life with an inner strength and quiet calm that only comes from Him.

We read of it in Hebrews 10:35, "Cast not away therefore your confidence, which hath great recompence of reward." Again in Philippians 1:6, "Being confident of this very thing, that he which hath begun a good work in you will perform *it* until the day of Jesus Christ."

This is what Jesus had when we read, "Looking unto Jesus the author and finisher of our faith; who for the joy that was set before him endured the cross, despising the shame, and is set down at the right hand of the throne of God" (Hebrews 12:2). He endured the cross because of the joy. He pressed forward through the pain because He understood the prize.

This Christ-based *confidence* compels us forward through resistance. It gives quiet, inner strength that cannot be touched by the unpredictability of life. This confidence gives courage to endure the temporary because of the value of the eternal. It so highly values the prize that the cost becomes merely a "light affliction."

Friend, you cannot avoid pain in life. It is impossible. Life is unpredictable, uncertain, and uncontrollable. That's just the nature of it. You cannot change this any more than you can change the color of the sky or the temperature of the sun. It's a fact. But God hasn't sent you into this life without the resources available to endure the pain and triumph in the trials. He offers you an enduring confidence in Christ and He promises you a great recompense of reward. He promises you that every circumstance is working together for your ultimate good, and He invites you to trust Him, rest in Him, and endure with Him. Let's face it—without God, life is scary. But with Him, life takes on a quiet, calm assurance.

This confidence is the opposite of fear. In fact, it's the cure for fear. Paul wrote in 2 Timothy 1:7, "For God hath not given us the spirit of fear; but of power, and of love, and of a sound mind." While millions of people your age look at life and freeze with fear, you can step forward with a sound mind, the love of God, and the power of Christ. While the world mocks your Christian values, they will simultaneously be wondering with admiration. They will be curious where you get this unparalleled strength and perspective. While your religion will seem strange to them, your fearless confidence will be envied.

Paul referenced two kinds of battles that he endured.

The most important was a battle within. Romans chapter 7 reveals Paul's struggle with the flesh versus the Spirit. He writes about his desires within conflicting with his performance. He basically says, I don't do the things I want to do, and I do the things I don't want to do. At the end of the chapter he declares, "O wretched man that I am! who shall deliver me from the body of this death?" (Romans 7:24). To paraphrase—this is too hard! I can't do this! I'm a loser! But then he declares, "I thank God through Jesus Christ our Lord..." (Romans 7:25). He realized that the battle within was the design of God, and he resolved to fight that battle in the power of Christ.

Your Christian life is first a battle within. That battle isn't to be quit. It's to be fought and endured. You will win some and lose some, but the winning is in the fighting. The victory is found in enduring—keeping your eye on the prize. You may feel at times like you're failing, but if you're still fighting, you're winning. That's the promise of Christ. "But thanks be to God, which giveth us the victory through our Lord Jesus Christ" (1 Corinthians 15:57).

The second battle was the battle without. This is what Paul referenced about being persecuted, cast down, etc. Several times in the New Testament he recounts stories of being stoned, beaten, shipwrecked, and imprisoned. Through it all he endured. He found calm, confidence in Christ and he kept his eye on the prize.

Last night, my daughter had another meltdown. This time it wasn't about being four again. It was about teeth. She recently found out that her teeth will soon become loose and fall out. This was devastating news to her. I mean, we had a major emotional crisis at our kitchen table over this. She bit on a fork, felt her front tooth shift slightly, and immediately burst into tearful panic—you would have thought she chopped her arm off or something.

Isn't it wonderful how God created little-girl-screams to grind so perfectly against our spinal cord? Let's just say, her outburst got my attention. I walked to her chair, set her on the table, looked into her eyes and said, "Haylee, what's the matter?"

Tears streaming, chest heaving, new glasses set perfectly on her face, she looked at me with the most pitiful, fear-filled face that I have ever seen. She captured her emotions just long enough to whimper, "My teeth are going to fall out..." and then she lost it again.

You already know I'm not good with these situations. The first thing I did was laugh. Fortunately my wife was laughing too, so that makes it okay. But Haylee was offended at our laughter and only cried louder and longer. I tried hard to gather my composure, so I could help her gather hers. Plus, my spinal cord couldn't take much more.

I cupped her cute little face in my hands, dried her tears with my t-shirt, and began to explain to her about losing teeth. I tried everything. I told her they won't hurt. I showed her mine, Mom's, Lance's, Larry's and explained how they all grew back. I told her how ridiculous she would look if she grew up with baby teeth—gigantic head, itty-bitty teeth. She almost laughed at that one. But still she cried. Her fear was enormous, and the more she questioned the more I understood.

"But what if they all fall out at once?" she spoke in the most desperate tones, "Then I won't be able to eat anything. What if they all fall out but one, then I will only have one tooth! What if they don't grow back! They bleed when they fall out. I saw an old man at Wal-Mart whose tooth didn't grow back...." On and on her argument went. It wasn't until money came into the issue that losing teeth became bearable. Oh, you mean they not only grow back, but I get money when they fall out? Cool!

After a few moments, she settled down and accepted the idea that losing teeth is inevitable.

When you realize that pain in life is inevitable, the first reaction of the heart is *fear*. But fearing life is something like fearing the loss of teeth. Think back for a moment. Did you fear losing teeth? Probably not for long. There were moments of slight pain, even a little blood and discomfort—but then money entered the picture. I know kids who went around trying to get teeth knocked out just so they could make a few bucks from the "tooth fairy."

This morning, I was awakened from a short night's sleep by a six-year-old girl in a pink nightgown. She climbed up next to my pillow, dangled her hair in my eyes, kissed my cheek, and softly said, "Ten dollars?"

Trying to get my brain in gear, I turned over, looked at her and said, "What?"

"When I lose a tooth...can I get ten dollars?" Then she smiled and laughed.

"Ten dollars! You've got to be kidding. How about five?"

Deal. She smiled, climbed out of bed, and started looking forward to the prize. I rolled over, laughed, and wished I could hit the snooze button for three more hours.

Haylee is now keeping her eye on the prize. The prize makes losing teeth bearable—endurable.

*You* were the prize that made the cross bearable for Jesus. *He* is the prize that makes life bearable for you!

You'll never be able to remove the pain from life. You'll never avoid discomfort completely. You will be opposed. The Christian life is a battle to be fought, a marathon to be endured, and a mission to be accomplished. Your enemy will relentlessly try to knock your teeth out. He is ruthless. Every good thing you attempt in life will be opposed. Every right decision will be tested. Every right thing will be resisted. Nothing moves forward without friction.

Keep your eye on the prize.

Peter discovered this confidence, "But the God of all grace, who hath called us unto his eternal glory by Christ Jesus, after that ye have suffered a while, make you perfect, stablish, strengthen, settle you" (1 Peter 5:10). And so did Jesus' brother, "Knowing this, that the trying of your faith worketh patience. But let patience have her perfect work, that ye may be perfect and entire, wanting nothing" (James 1:3–4).

You can have this confidence too!

## Finishing Requires Renewal

The final quality that Paul exhibited in finishing his course is renewal. Another word for this is balance. He understood how God created life to function and he lived within those boundaries. If you want to *finish*, pay attention. This is vital.

Paul wrote that we are made up of three parts—"And the very God of peace sanctify you wholly; and I pray God your whole spirit and soul and body be preserved blameless unto the coming of our Lord Jesus Christ" (1 Thessalonians 5:23). This principle is clear in many other Scriptures. When God created those three components of your being (spirit, soul, and body), He created them with natural cycles and needs. For instance, you know already that your body requires an average of seven to eight hours of sleep per night. (And if you're one of those rare people who can get by with four hours a night and be just fine, I don't like you.)

When your body is tired, you rest it. When it's hungry, you feed it. When it's sick, you treat it. When it's thirsty, you fill it. You know how to care for your body. Perhaps you don't do it very well, but at least you know how to read the signals and what to do in response.

This is not always the case with your soul and spirit, which is why I share this with you. I see many young adults charge forward in life only to fail because of this basic principle of renewal. While you are passionate about pressing forward and living a focused life, you must also be passionate about maintaining a healthy balance. You must understand principles of spiritual renewal. The Christian life is a marathon, and every marathon runner knows how to set a *sustainable pace*.

You must know that it is possible to get tired in your soul and spirit—the Bible calls this *weariness*. "And let us not be weary in well doing: for in due season we shall reap, if we faint not" (Galatians 6:9). This is a rotten feeling. When your soul is weary you tend to stop caring about important things. You get apathetic—spiritually numb. You wonder why you're doing the things you're doing. These are dangerous seasons when many adults make bad decisions. These are times when Satan takes advantage of your weariness and uses it against you. This is what he did with Jesus when he tempted Him in the wilderness.

I want to warn you. In your passionate commitment to Christ, you will occasionally become weary. You can't avoid it. But you can properly respond to weariness.

God's cure for weariness is *renewal*. "For which cause we faint not; but though our outward man perish, yet the inward man is renewed day by day" (2 Corinthians 4:16). There is such a thing as rest for your soul and spirit—and you must learn to read the signals of spiritual weariness and then learn to rest your soul in God. "He giveth power to the faint; and to them that have no might he increaseth strength. Even the youths shall faint and be weary, and the young men shall utterly fall: But they that wait upon the LORD shall renew their strength; they shall mount up with wings as eagles; they shall run, and not be weary; and they shall walk, and not faint" (Isaiah 40:29-31). Everyone gets weary—even the youths—but God's cure is His renewing strength to those who wait upon Him.

> *God's cure for weariness is renewal.*

I wish I understood this earlier in life, but seasons of weariness are just that—seasons. I have entered and exited more than I care to remember. These are times when circumstances, pressure, and busyness bring your soul to emptiness. Often they are times when you've neglected your walk with Christ or when you've filled your schedule with too much. When your soul grows weary, your reasoning becomes flawed, your heart becomes calloused, and your vision becomes foggy. If you're not careful you will misread the signals and self-destruct. It would be like jumping off a cliff because you're tired, when all you really need is a good night's sleep. Weariness is deceptive. It hides beneath the surface of life and impacts your spirit and your perspective. Like a fun-house mirror, it distorts reality and causes error.

The Apostle Paul understood weariness and how to deal with it. He knew how to rest his soul in God. David encouraged himself in the Lord. God sent an angel and birds to minister to Elijah. Throughout Scripture you'll find weary souls renewing their strength in God. And He invites you to do the same. This is why you must cultivate your passion for God. Only with Him can you rest your soul and renew your strength.

For me the key to renewal has been two simple things. The first is to simply wait. Tunnels have beginnings and ends. I don't freak out when I'm going through one. I just anticipate that it will end. (And sometimes I honk the horn all the way through.) This is how you must handle weariness. Don't quit. Just wait. The second is to spend time with God—read His Word, talk to Him, read good books, listen to Christ-honoring music, really worship in church, listen to teaching and preaching. There are a thousand ways to spend time with God in renewing your spirit. Remember, waiting on God is not passive, but active.

When your soul grows weary, and your vision dim, don't panic. Look hard at your life, your schedule, your load and ask yourself—am I *sprinting* or *marathoning*? Is my pace *healthy* or *destructive*? Are my soul and spirit weary? If so, make the changes you must make to bring balance and spiritual renewal back to your heart. In time, it will be as though God personally breathed fresh air into your spiritual lungs. He will renew your strength. Just don't jump off a cliff before He does!

Derek Redmond is a great runner, but he's an even greater finisher. Derek will be forever remembered for his staggering performance in the 400-meter men's semifinals during the summer Olympics of 1992 in Barcelona, Spain.

After years of training, persistence, and self-discipline, Derek was competing on the world stage. His dream had become a reality. Halfway through this 400-meter race, Derek pulled a hamstring muscle and collapsed on the track. Writhing in pain, he watched the other runners quickly pass him and his dream of winning die. But staying down wasn't in Derek's blood. Though winning was out of the question, finishing wasn't.

As the medical crew arrived with a stretcher, Derek said, "There's no way I'm getting on that stretcher. I'm going to finish my race."

In a stadium packed with 65,000 fans, and with millions viewing around the world, Derek slowly struggled to his feet. In spite of the agonizing pain, he began hobbling towards the finish line in last place. Tears streamed down his face as his heart filled with disappointment. Yet, he was determined to finish the race.

At that point, a large man in the top row of the stands began to bound towards the track. It was Jim Redmond, Derek's father. Disregarding security guards, running over people, determined that no one would stop him, he ran to his son's side. At first Derek tried to push him away, not realizing it was his father. He thought someone was trying to get him to quit the race.

"Derek, it's me."

Recognizing that familiar voice, Derek said, "Dad, I've got to finish the race."

"If you're gonna finish the race, then we'll finish it together." With those words, his father took his son in his arms and together they began to hobble down the track.

By this time, the other runners had completed the race and the crowd realized that Derek wasn't hobbling off the track—he was hobbling towards the finish line on one leg with his father at his side. In total disbelief, 65,000 fans stood to their feet and began to cheer. The roar of the crowd increased with every painful step.

Approaching the finish line, Jim Redmond stepped aside to allow Derek to cross by himself. The crowd exploded in thunderous applause and emotional release. Derek collapsed in his father's embrace and both wept—along with 65,000 fans and millions of viewers.

Derek had finished the race and the world would never forget it!

Derek Redmond had two things that made him a finisher that day. First, he had a passion to finish. In spite of pain and disappointment, he pressed forward. It wasn't the crowd that compelled him forward. It was his heart. He was passionate about getting across that finish line. Second, he had a father who helped him—a man who refused to remain in the stands and watch his son suffer. He spanned the distance and braved Olympic security to get to his son. Nothing could hold him back.

My friend, you are running a race! That race has a finish line. Get it in your mind. You will not run forever. Rest is coming! Keep the end in view. Envision crossing that line into the welcoming arms of your Heavenly Father.

As you run your race, you will face pain. Finishing requires patience, contentment, enduring confidence, and renewal. At times you will be hurt and sometimes you will fail. At times the pain may be so overwhelming, all you can do is cry. At times you will need a long night's sleep and renewed strength. But you must *refuse* to be carried off the track in a stretcher. You must have a passion to finish the race.

In the grandstands of Heaven a great cloud of witnesses cheers you on. Bounding through security guards and barricades, your Heavenly Father cannot stay in the stands and watch you suffer! He runs to your side, holds you in His arms, and bears you up in His strength. He gives you courage to press forward. He offers His life to help you embrace yours. He knows your pain. His eye is on the prize, and He will see you safely home. Whether you are running or hobbling, He will strengthen you until you cross the finish line, where you will collapse in His eternal embrace—forever grateful that you *finished*.

You will be tired, breathless, tearful, and wounded. You will have been beaten up by battles, scarred by sin, and tried by fires. But you will face your Father as a finisher. You will say with the Apostle Paul—I pressed toward the mark; I kept the faith; I finished my course!

# THE BEST LIFE

*Choosing the Path of Most Resistance*

This book has been a journey for both of us. Thank you for reading. The preparation has been years in the making. The trends I'm seeing in culture are verified in secular research. They are alarming. I have done my best to compel you to go forward with courage and passion. You only have one life—you must live it well.

In these pages, you have been challenged to overcome immaturity, irresponsibility, rebellion, ignorance, and folly. You have been encouraged to pursue the fulfilling rewards of God's plan for your life—a life of significance, the great gifts of God, and the rewards of a faithful steward. Finally, we have studied three godly passions of successful adulthood—a passion for God, a passion for God's perfect will, and a passion to finish your course.

Articulating these values and principles has been a challenge. There is so much truth to learn from God's Word. I feel that we have barely scratched the surface. But I hope your interest is piqued. I hope your heart is hungry for God, for the life He purposes, and for the rewards He promises.

One of the overriding messages of this book is that the path of *most resistance* is the path of *best blessings*. While most in culture are seeking the path of least resistance, I pray that you will choose a different path. Swim upstream. Embrace your life; seize the day; and passionately live out God's purpose. The path of most resistance leads to the best life!

In closing, I want to share the story of a hero of mine. He was perhaps the youngest and most mature adult that I've ever seen embrace these principles and live them out to the fullest. His name is Edward.

Edward Bordell was eight years old in 1995, when his family moved to Costa Rica as missionaries. Later that year, after a series of health struggles and tests, he was diagnosed with leukemia. Immediately his family returned to Northern California for emergency medical treatment, and by a miraculous answer to prayer, Edward was accepted for treatment at the Stanford Medical Center in Palo Alto, California.

Not even knowing what leukemia was at the time, Edward accepted God's providence in his life willingly, and he courageously began weekly chemotherapy treatments. For fourteen months, Edward endured hospital stays, hair loss, pain, fevers, headaches, and physical exhaustion. He intentionally scheduled the treatments on Wednesday so that by Sunday he would be strong enough to attend church with his family. Even at eight years old, Edward loved God passionately and trusted Him with the future.

> *The path of most resistance is the path of best blessings.*

Fourteen months later, Edward's cancer went into remission, and his family returned to the mission field where he continued to receive treatment while he served God with his father. The doctors told him that five years was the goal. If the cancer stayed in remission for five years, it most likely would never return. Time does not permit me to tell all the ways that God sustained Edward and his family or all the prayers that He specifically answered along the way. These stories alone could fill a book. The most amazing part of the story is Edward's trust in God. His relationship with God ran deep and strong. At an amazingly young age, he had grown spiritual roots that anchored him during a very unpredictable time of life.

Four years on the mission field came and went with no sign of relapse. Edward and his family were prayerfully hopeful as January of 2000 approached. Now thirteen, Edward was attending a teen camp with his youth group in the jungles of Costa Rica. He wasn't feeling well—his bones ached, walking and running were difficult, and he knew in his heart that the cancer had returned. Without saying much to his family about how he felt, he determined to enjoy camp. He had a feeling that this would be his last youth activity in Costa Rica, and he wanted to enjoy it to the fullest. In his father's words, "He pushed himself to the limit to enjoy to the most of his ability."

At thirteen years of age, Edward had a passion to enjoy and savor life. He valued every day, every moment, and every opportunity. Every day since 1995 was a gift, and he recognized God as the giver.

A few days and a few tests later, the Bordells were headed back to the states for another battle against the leukemia that had relapsed in Edward's body. The protocol was to begin an aggressive two-year treatment plan that would hopefully drive the cancer back into remission, but the doctors didn't give much hope. Remission at this point was unlikely.

For two more years, Edward received aggressive chemo treatments, which brought on physical, emotional, and spiritual struggles that are difficult to describe. He endured enormous physical pain, hair loss, bodily weakness, sleeplessness, and dozens of other discomforts and physical struggles. Chemotherapy basically poisons the body in an effort to kill cancer, and as a result Edward's life became a living torment. His emotions were unpredictable, severe headaches were frequent, and many nights he couldn't sleep at all.

But Edward trusted in God. When life was unpredictable, painful, and exhausting, Edward chose a different path "across the pavement." Let me tell you about Edward's heart.

Though his body was weak and his sickness severe—his heart was just fine. His heart knew God. His heart trusted God. His heart clung to God during the darkest hours of life.

Second Chronicles 16:9 says, "For the eyes of the LORD run to and fro throughout the whole earth, to shew himself strong in the behalf of them whose heart is perfect toward him...." Edward's heart was perfect towards God.

Edward never wanted to burden anyone with his illness—especially his family. He would hide his pain as much as possible. He was a joyful, fun-loving teenager and didn't like the idea of being the center of attention. He was humble and sincere, and he savored every moment of life that God gave him.

*Wrap your arms around God and His purpose and don't ever let go.*

Because he couldn't sleep, he chose to battle his cancer alone with God during the night hours. While his family was asleep, Edward would spend his nights listening to godly music, reading the Word of God, pouring out his heart in prayer, and fighting his spiritual battles privately. Oftentimes his father or mother would awaken and find Edward in his room, one light on, reading God's Word and walking with God in the night hours.

While most kids his age were overdosing on fun, video games, and TV, Edward was overdosing on God. Alone in the night he discovered a strength that only God could give him, and when the sun came up each day, his soul struggle was set aside so that he could minister to his family. He gave himself to others. He made every effort to be happy, entertaining, and encouraging. He comforted his siblings, served his parents, and trusted his God.

By August of 2002, Edward's fifteenth birthday had come and gone. His body had become undeniably weak— but his heart had grown unbelievably strong. You cannot spend that much time with God without growing strong and deep in His grace. Doctors and psychologists had basically stopped trying to counsel Edward because he usually ended up trying to counsel *them*! They didn't understand where his strength came from.

Becoming increasingly weaker, Edward decided it would be easiest on his family if he was checked into the hospital. No one stopped praying for a miracle, and everyone knew that God could heal Edward if He chose to. But Edward was not afraid of death.

With great courage, he made this statement on the Saturday that he checked into the hospital at Stanford University, "Dad, by Friday at noon I'm out of here. I'm either flying out by wing or walking out in shoes."

During those few days, friends and family came to see Edward to try to encourage him. Yet, every one of them would tell you, it was the other way around! He encouraged them! Then in moments alone with his parents, he began to plan his memorial service. He told his parents, "It's not going to be morbid. It's going to be upbeat because going home to Heaven is an upbeat thing! I feel bad for your suffering, but one day, we all will be together again!"

By 9:00 PM Thursday, Edward's pain was so bad that he could not lay down in bed. The doctors offered him morphine, but he refused. He knew that the morphine would remove the pain, but along with it make him semi-comatose. Edward preferred to be awake *with* the pain than *asleep* without it. He didn't want to sleep his life away, he wanted to be awake for every visitor, and alert for every moment—especially for his mother. To him, every moment was a gift, even if it involved pain.

Somewhere near 11:00 PM Thursday, Edward's organs were enlarging and his pain was so bad that he could only sit up, but he wasn't strong enough to hold himself up. So, Edward's father, Ed Sr., found a spot on the edge of the bed, embraced his son, and held him upright through the night. Together they prayed, sang, and encouraged each other. Sometime during the night Edward's communication was reduced to groans, his breathing was labored and he often coughed up blood—but he responded to every word his father said. He was well aware of what was happening and where he was headed, and throughout the entire seven-year battle he had never complained one time.

Some months prior, during one of his nights with God, he had chosen a life verse, "The LORD is good, a strong hold in the day of trouble; and he knoweth them that trust in him" (Nahum 1:7).

For thirteen hours, Edward rested on his earthly father for *physical* strength just as he had rested on his Heavenly Father for *spiritual* strength. His last seven years were spent in God's embrace, and his last thirteen hours in his father's embrace. Sometime during that last night he told his dad to "take care of Mom." Even then he was thinking of others, just as Jesus did from the cross.

As the sun rose that Friday morning, Edward's deadline for leaving the hospital was only hours away. Still resting in his father's arms, he was mostly out of consciousness. As the noon hour approached, Ed Sr. felt it best to pray. His pastor prayed, and then he prayed—together they asked the Lord to do His will and take Edward to Heaven.

Ed Sr. had a difficult time explaining this next experience, but as he closed in prayer, he immediately sensed that Edward was gone—"out of here on wings" as he had put it. Still holding his son, he looked at his wife and pastor and said, "Well, that's it." The red light and the alarm on Edward's heart monitor went off and Ed Sr. gently laid his son back on the bed.

Edward Bordell embraced life with passion and faced his future with courage. He savored every moment, treasured every relationship, and trusted His God every step of the way. By nine, he had grown up, by thirteen he had a passion for God, and by fifteen he had finished his course with joy.

Why finish this book with Edward's story? Let me put it into perspective.

*Part one*—Edward had no interest in folly. He chose wisdom! He chose to understand life! He was the farthest thing from rebellious, immature, or irresponsible. He realized early that life had a purpose, that God was good, and that the future was precious. Cancer changed his whole perspective.

*Part two*—Edward walked through life with his head up! He lived for eternal rewards, he savored every small thing as an awesome gift from God, and he made his life count! He lived to serve God, to help others know Christ, and to honor his family. He found significance with God. I submit to you that Edward had more significance in his short fifteen years than most people have in a lifetime.

*Part three*—Edward fell in love with God. He passionately walked with God and desired to know Him. He found strength, joy, and hope during his private time with his Heavenly Father. He had a passion for God's will and lived with a heart of surrender. Indeed, he embraced his very *struggle* as God's perfect will, and delighted in living out God's purpose by faith. And Edward had a passion to finish his course. To his last moments in refusing morphine, in praying and singing with his father and not wanting to burden his mother—he displayed unspeakable commitment to Christ and a passion to finish his course with joy.

Edward embodied the principles of this book better than any human being I've ever seen, and he did it all before his sixteenth birthday.

So often as a student ministries pastor, I challenge twenty-year-olds to brave adulthood. I encourage young adults to embrace life and to live it with purpose. I compel them to fall in love with God and to pursue Him with passion. And so often, they are too concerned with their cell phones, their new car, their next paycheck, and their tans to care much about anything else. So often they look to the future with dread and fear, and they try to freeze in time—to stay teen-ish through their twenties and beyond.

> *The best life is the life God created you to live.*

I pray that these pages have pulled back the curtain of your heart and exposed any folly that may be found there. I pray that they have pulled back the curtain of eternity and exposed the wonderful rewards and gifts that God desires to give you. And I pray that they have pulled back the curtain of your future and infused passion into your heart.

The best life is the life God created you to live—Edward Bordell proved it! But it's also the path of most resistance. God didn't create you to live a resistance-free life, He created you to fulfill a very specific purpose in His plan. That plan involves resistance, but it also involves enormous rewards. Lift up your head and see the big picture.

Say "no" to that perpetual state of limbo. Say "no" to fear and immaturity. Say "no" to irresponsibility and folly. Wrap your arms around God and His purpose and don't ever let go. Growing up is a pain, but it's an AWESOME pain and it's well worth it!

The formula is quite simple really—*choose the path of most resistance; live the best life.*

So there you are, looking at the land of adulthood just across the parking lot of maturity. Others have tried to cross, and they've been burned. It scares you. It scared me too. That's a good thing, because you don't want to take that route! You *should be* scared of venturing into life *your own* way. It doesn't work. But that's no excuse not to get across. You *must.* You can't avoid the future. You can't avoid adulthood. Hopefully by now, you don't *want to*! There are too many rewards, too much purpose, and too great a future to pass up!

And along comes a Heavenly Father. He extends His hand in your direction. He offers to carry you across the parking lot of maturity. He offers to be everything you need and to give your heart everything it craves. He is your designer—no one knows you like He does and no one loves you like He does. Like Edward's father, He will hold you up for the rest of your life just because He loves you.

You're not sure you can trust Him. His plan scares you. His will makes you nervous. But a little time with Him will reveal the kindness in His eyes, the goodness of His heart, and the rewards of His way. If you would just get to know Him, you would trust His heart. He seems scary from a distance, but once you get over the size of His power, you'll fall in love with Him.

He's standing there waiting for your decision—His nail-pierced hand is extended your way. His huge heart is madly in love with you. He wants to be your Father. He wants to guide you, bless you, use you, and care for you.

Do you "risk" trusting Him or do you follow the crowd?

Do you choose His goodness or your own foolishness?

Do you grab His hand with courage or do you decide to go it alone?

What will you do with your life quest?

Edward Bordell wrapped his arms around his father and never let go.

Now you go and do the same.

*The LORD is good, a strong hold in the day of trouble; and he knoweth them that trust in him.*

—Nahum 1:7

# NOTES

*Quotes, references, and illustrations were taken from the following:*

Apter, Terri. *The Myth of Maturity*. New York and London: W.W. Norton & Company, 2001. 18.

Arnett, Jeffrey Jensen. *Emerging Adulthood: the Winding Road From the Late Teens Through the Twenties*. New York: Oxford UP, 2004

Cote, James. *Arrested Adulthood: the Changing Nature of Maturity and Identity*. New York and London: New York UP, 2000.

Marquardt, Elizabeth. "New Reasons to Stay Together." *Reader's Digest* June 2006: 161–163.

Petre, Caitlin. "The Lessons I Didn't Learn in College." *Newsweek* 13 Nov. 2006: 20–21.

**Twixters**
Grossman, Lev. "Grow Up? Not So Fast." *TIME Magazine* 24 Jan. 2005: 42–54.

**Bridge Jumping**
Burdi, Jerome. "Father Jumps Off Intracoastal Bridge with Daughter, 10, to Cure Her Fear of Heights." South Florida Sun-Sentinel, 13 Sept. 2006. 27 Oct. 2006 <www.sun-sentinel.com>.

**Air Force One**
"Internet Hoaxers Explain Air Force One Prank." MSNBC. 21 Apr. 2006. 28 Oct. 2006 <http://www.msnbc.msn.com/id/12425846>.

**Balloons and Lawn Chair**
"Larry Walters." Wikipedia. 23 Oct. 2006. Wikimedia Foundation, Inc. 27 Oct. 2006 <http://en.wikipedia.org>.

**Gold Rush**
"John Sutter." Wikipedia. 24 Oct. 2006. Wikimedia Foundation, Inc. 28 Oct. 2006 <http://en.wikipedia.org>.

"Life of John Augustus Sutter 1803–1880." SCORE. CTAP and CCSESA. 28 Oct. 2006 <http://score.rims.k12.ca.us/activity/suttersfort/pages/sutter.html>.

Sutter, John A. "The Discovery of Gold in California." The Virtual Museum of the City of San Fransisco. Nov. 1857. 28 Oct. 2006 <http://www.sfmuseum.org/hist2/gold.html>.

**Red Paper Clip**
Colligan, Doug. "Trading Up." *Reader's Digest* Nov. 2006. 28 Oct. 2006 <www.rd.com>.

"One Red Paperclip." Wikipedia. 26 Oct. 2006. Wikimedia Foundation, Inc. 28 Oct. 2006 <http://en.wikipedia.org/wiki/One_red_paperclip>.

## Surfer

Howard, Jake. "Daily Dale Webster Achieves Goal." *Surfer Magazine*. 28 Oct. 2006 <http://www.surfermag.com/features/daleweb/>.

"Dale Webster: the Man of a Million Waves." Globe Visions. 28 Oct. 2006 <http://www.globevisions.com/english/DaleWebster/index_DaleWebster.htm>.

"Riding the Crest of a (Long) Wave." *Taipei Times*, 3 Mar. 2004. 28 Oct. 2006 <http://www.taipeitimes.com>.

## Erie Pizza Delivery

"Brian Wells." Wikipedia. 25 Oct. 2006. Wikimedia Foundation, Inc. 14 Nov. 2006 <http://en.wikipedia.org>.

McGraw, Seamus. "The Erie Collar Bomber." Crime Library. Courtroom Television Network. 14 Nov. 2006 <http://www.crimelibrary.com/notorious_murders/famous/erie_collar_bomber/index.html>

## Chris McCandless—Hitchhiking to Alaska

"Christopher McCandless." Wikipedia. 3 Nov. 2006. Wikimedia Foundation, Inc. 11 Nov. 2006 <http://en.wikipedia.org>.

## Derek Redmond—Crossing the Finish Line

Weinberg, Rick. "Derek and Dad Finish Olympic 400 Together." *Sports Illustrated*. 28 Oct. 2006 <http://sports.espn.go.com/espn/espn25/story?page=moments/94>.

"Derek Redmond." Wikipedia. 18 Aug. 2006. Wikimedia Foundation, Inc. 28 Oct. 2006 <http://en.wikipedia.org/wiki/Derek_Redmond>.

# ABOUT THE AUTHOR

**CARY SCHMIDT** serves as the senior pastor of Emmanual Baptist Church in Newington, Connecticut. He and his wife Dana have three children and enjoy serving the Lord and spending time together as a family. Cary's books include *Passionate Parenting, Off Script*, and others.

You can connect with Cary through his blog, Twitter, and Facebook:

caryschmidt.com
twitter.com/CarySchmidt
facebook.com/schmidtcary

# Other books by Cary Schmidt
# from Striving Together Publications

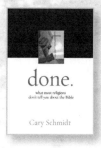

### done.
This minibook explains the Gospel in crystal clear terms. The reader will journey step by step through biblical reasoning that concludes at the Cross and a moment of decision. (100 pages, mini paperback)

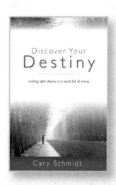

### Discover Your Destiny
What every young adult needs to know about making right choices in a world full of wrong! This book will help anyone, young or old to discover the perfect will of God for their lives. (280 pages, paperback)

### Just Friends
This book will help you protect your heart as you journey through the dangerous minefields of young emotions and early attractions. And it will help you understand the biblical principles that will ultimately lead you to true love and a "wonderful someday." Includes a study guide for personal application! (264 pages, paperback)

strivingtogether.com

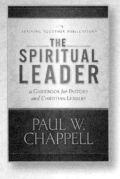
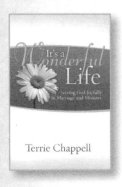
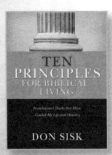

# Visit us online

strivingtogether.com

wcbc.edu